THE WORLD ART TOUR

Clothing and Fashion

Architecture

Clothing and Fashion

Culinary Arts

Dance

Decorative Arts

Drawing and Painting

Festivals

Sculpture

THE WORLD ART TOUR
Clothing and Fashion

BY Amy Sterling Casil

MASON CREST
Philadelphia • Miami

Mason Crest
450 Parkway Drive, Suite D
Broomall, PA 19008
(866) MCP-BOOK (toll free)
www.masoncrest.com

Printed in the United States of America

First printing
9 8 7 6 5 4 3 2 1

Series ISBN: 978-1-4222-4283-4
Hardcover ISBN: 978-1-4222-4285-8
E-book ISBN: 978-1-4222-7532-0

Cataloging-in-Publication Data is available on file
at the Library of Congress.

Developed and Produced by Print Matters Productions, Inc.
(www.printmattersinc.com)

Cover and Interior Design by Tom Carling, Carling Design, Inc.

CONTENTS

Introduction.. 6

Key Terms.. 8

1 Africa.. 9

2 Asia.. 21

3 Europe.. 33

4 Latin America and the Caribbean............. 45

5 Middle East.. 57

6 North America 69

7 Oceania... 81

Further Reading & Internet Resources........................... 94

Index 95

Author's Biography & Credits...................................... 96

INTRODUCTION

According to genetic studies of lice that live in human clothing—compared to lice that live on our heads—the two species began to differ from each other about 170,000 years ago. What this shows is that people have worn clothing at least since that time. There's no way to know what types of clothing people wore so long ago, but archaeologists have given us a glimpse of sophisticated clothes worn by ancient Egyptians, as well as fabrics, weaving, and clothing construction techniques that are diverse—and at times surprisingly similar—around the ancient world.

Early humans probably wore clothes to protect themselves from extreme weather and also for utility, such as carrying needed items or children. One of the oldest objects of clothing was likely a wrap that helped parents to carry babies safely.

People wear clothing for many reasons. The first reason is practical: When humans lost body hair, they needed protection from the elements that fur, feathers, or scales provide for animals. Second, just as birds like the peacock display their extraordinary tail feathers to attract a mate, humans use clothing to attract others. Clothing also helps to establish identities and jobs. A crossing guard, for example, wears a high-visibility vest and carries a sign. Rank, status, and roles in society are also indicated through clothing. Finally, the feeling of human modesty influences many choices in clothing, from people who are comfortable wearing a tiny loincloth or merely painted body decorations to those who want to cover all of their body except their hands and face.

Clothing's practical and social aspects influence style and fashion, but they don't dictate fashion. These are sometimes confused. *Style* refers to an individual's choice of clothing and how people choose to groom their hair, makeup, nails, and other personal characteristics. *Fashion*, on the other hand, is a creative art form practiced at a high level on every continent. Though "the passing fashion" may be a trend or fad that is popular for a short time, the fashion industry at its highest levels involves knowledge of human nature, the human body, color, textiles, and innovative materials and construction that goes far beyond traditional weaving, sewing, and fitting.

The fashion industry as it is known today emerged in France in the nineteenth century with the first fashion design firm: the House of Worth. Every continent has its own fashion tradition, and many of these customs reflect the society, climate, natural resources, religion, and culture of the people that follow them.

Africa, the birthplace of humanity and a diverse continent with 55 different countries and more than 2,000 languages, is the site of many emerging fashion designers and a world design capital: Cape Town, South Africa. The diverse clothing and style traditions of Africa caught the world's attention with the 2018 release of the film *Black Panther*. Designer Ruth E. Carter created the film's stunning costumes based on thousands of hours of research and study to blend African regional clothing.

The oldest known pants, designed for horseback riding, were discovered in a 5,000-year-old grave in China, which is the home of the world's most coveted and luxurious fabric: silk. The manufacture of silk was a closely guarded secret in China for thousands of years, but the secret is now "out," and school classrooms worldwide grow silkworms to watch them create their delicate cocoons and emerge as moths.

Japanese traditional clothing has given the world the beautiful kimono. Today's Japanese youth fashion culture influences world designers and street fashion around the globe. India, the birthplace of cotton, is home to one of the most colorful, vibrant fashion cultures in the world. India's Holi festival celebrates the coming of spring with an endless variety of colors in pigments that are literally sprinkled on festivalgoers throughout the streets.

Formal fashion and haute couture originated in Europe, where Paris, Milan, and London vie for the title of fashion capital each year. We may think that the ancient Greeks and Romans exclusively wore white togas, but recent research shows their clothing was more diverse than statues show and was bursting with vibrant colors and intricate woven designs. Luxury fabrics and materials entered European households in the Middle Ages and haven't left. Although fashion is truly worldwide in the twenty-first century, Paris is still the birthplace of haute couture and the pioneer of designer *prêt-à-porter*, or ready-to-wear clothing.

In the twentieth century, New York rose as a new fashion capital, and the daring decade of the 1920s gave rise to vast changes in women's fashion worldwide. "Western" clothing, worn around the world today, from blue jeans to T-shirts, came from the U.S. fashion industry. Hollywood glamour is reflected in Bollywood and other film industries worldwide. U.S. technological advances provided most of the world's synthetic fabrics, from nylon to Spandex and today's high-tech performance fabrics.

When we look at bikinis on Australia's Bondi Beach or revealing eveningwear from some of South America's top designers, it may be difficult to remember that not every person wants to reveal all parts of their body in public. Islamic modesty has led to the rise of modest fashion, bringing the hijab—an article of clothing worn due to religious and cultural beliefs—into the world of fashion. We know one thing for certain: Some aspects of clothing have remained the same for thousands of years, but fashion as an art form is ever-changing.

KEY TERMS

Bespoke: Tailored clothing made specifically for an individual, especially menswear.

Fashion industry: From designers to manufacturers and retailers, the industry that creates and sells clothing for personal style and adornment.

Formalwear: Clothing worn for ceremonial or important occasions.

Garment: An article of clothing (for any gender).

Haute couture: Exclusive custom-fitted clothing made by designers for elite clients.

Knit: The creation of cloth from a single thread using one or more needles.

Patterns: Cloth, plastic, or metal basic pieces that enable fabric to be cut and sewn into tailored clothing.

Prêt-à-porter: The French word for designer clothing that is mass-produced and sold in retail stores.

Printed fabric: Fabric with designs that are applied by external dyes or colors through blocks, stencils, rollers, or silkscreens.

Shawl: A woven or knitted scarf worn around the shoulders.

Silhouette: The outline or shape formed by a garment, especially a fitted suit or coat.

Sportswear: Clothing worn for athletic events or exercise.

Synthetic fabric: Fabric that is made from thread created by chemical processes, including nylon and polyester.

Tailoring: The process of cutting and fitting pieces of fabric to form a fitted garment and fit it to the body.

Tanning: The process of making animal skins durable, soft, and wearable.

Textiles: Cloth fabrics or other materials (like tapa cloth made from bark) used for clothing manufacture.

Tunic: A loose-fitting garment reaching to the mid-hip or knee.

Weaving: The process of making fabrics by alternating two or more horizontal and vertical threads (warp and weft).

CHAPTER ❶ AFRICA

Africa is considered the "birthplace of humanity," and 55 different countries make up the African Union today. The continent has 10 different regions and over 2,000 languages. Today's fashion trends and designers are emerging in every area, from South Africa's Cape Town, named the 2014 World Design Capital, to Dakar in Senegal, which is known as the "Paris of Africa."

KENTE: THE MOST FAMOUS WOVEN CLOTH

About 400 years ago, kente cloth, an iconic African fabric full of symbolism and meaning, was first woven in an Ashanti (or Asante) village called Bonwire. A legend about Anansi, the trickster spider, explains the origin of the woven cloth. Two brothers, Kurugu (or Karaban) and Ameyaw, went hunting and saw a spider, Anansi, weaving a web. Inspired by the web's intricacy, they returned home and wove the first kente cloth with intricate geometric patterns, using black and white fibers from the raffia tree.

The weavers presented their black and white cloth to the Ashanti king, who was very impressed. He said the cloth would be even more beautiful if woven in colors. A weaver called Akwasi Opoku–Agyeman experimented with tree bark dyes to create the basic kente colors: black, red, yellow, and green. Early kente cloth was exclusively royal—made for the king.

Locals use a strip loom to weave kente cloth.

Men wear a 24-strip-wide cloth, which is draped around their bodies and worn on one shoulder, while women wear combinations of five to 12 strips as skirts or dresses.

Kente's woven patterns include dozens of geometric themes combined in creative ways. The patterns have meanings, from alternating lozenge shapes that represent the king's eye, to zigzags that mean "life is not a straight path." Larger symbols include the Golden Stool, a symbol of absolute power, and purple and gold ribbons that stand for "your heart's desire." More than 10 colors are currently used in kente, and the meanings of patterns and geometric themes range from healing and harmony to love and good fortune.

Kente cloth continues to be woven on a strip loom, producing a narrow band of cloth. Kente weavers are primarily men. The bands of cloth are arranged and sewn together to create larger items of clothing. Men and women wear traditional kente cloth differently. Men usually wear a 24-strip-wide cloth, which is draped around the body and worn on one shoulder. Women wear combinations of five to 12 strips as skirts or dresses. The designs and patterns of kente cloth are known worldwide, and the fabric has been used in fashion design since the "kente revolution" of the 1980s and 1990s.

BLACK PANTHER'S ROOTS ARE IN REAL AFRICAN FASHION

In 2018, Marvel's *Black Panther* became the highest-earning superhero movie in history, earning more than $1 billion within 26 days of release. Set in the fictional African kingdom of Wakanda, the film's costumes inspired as much fandom as many of the characters and fictional conflicts. Award-winning costume designer Ruth E. Carter created Wakandan costumes for male and female characters inspired by historical and contemporary African culture, artisans, and fashion.

One of Carter's greatest challenges was designing costumes for the female warriors, Dora Milaje, who protect King T'Challa (Black Panther). Carter didn't want to put the warriors in bikinis or skimpy corsets—revealing Western-style outfits common in comic books created for young boys. After researching Africa's greatest warriors, she created costumes drawing on the red hues of Maasai clothing, beadwork, and metalwork. The final costumes were "feminine, masculine, beautiful and strong—and without showing an inch of skin," Carter told *Washington Post* writer Robin Givhan.

The costumes worn by the female warriors, Dora Milaje, of Black Panther were inspired by the red hues, beadwork, and metalwork of Maasai clothing.

The costumes for Black Panther were inspired by the clothing worn by the Maasai people.

Because Wakanda is a fictional African nation, *Black Panther*'s creative team, including Carter, chose clothing designs that reflected Wakandan ancestors, self- and community expression, and four words that Carter placed on her vision board: "Beautiful. Positive. Forward. Colorful." The African fabric traditions that Carter used for inspiration included Zulu, Maasai, Himba, and Dinka. She also incorpo-rated elements of several contemporary African designers, including Ghanaian designer Ozwald Boateng, Ikiré Jones's elaborate textiles, and MaXhosa by Laduma. Other inspirations include Afro-punk festivals and Congolese "Sapeurs," a tradition of fashion-conscious twenty-first-century "dandies" who live in the Central African cities of Kinshasa and Brazzaville.

Black Panther fashions have inspired a new interest in African clothing world-wide, including the United States. Traditional African clothing stores have been selling out of clothing from head wraps to *dashikis*. African American designers in many cities experienced increased sales of their clothing. "I think people are more comfortable wearing African clothing," said James Onabanjo, co-owner of an African clothing store in Georgia. "More African Americans . . . are trying to show off their heritage."

EARLY AFRICAN CLOTHING FROM TASSILI N'AJJER

Africa's climate extremes mean that early clothing from some areas, such as Central Africa, will never be known except through cultural legends and stories. But some ancient forms of clothing in Africa are known through rock art in the Tassili n'Ajjer region, deep in the Sahara Desert in present-day Algeria.

The Tassili rock art consists of more than 15,000 drawings and engravings dating back more than 9,000 years. The drawings show that in the ancient climate, which was as hot as much of Africa is today, people wore limited clothing. Some of the detailed Tassili paintings show dancing women with loincloths and intricate woven headdresses.

The paintings are so old that their complete spiritual meaning is unknown today, but some famous examples include a running horned woman who is wearing body paint, decorative armbands, and leg ornaments, and a dramatic horned headdress. The horns reflect the arrival of cattle between 4500 and 4000 BCE. Other horned figures depict shamans with goat or antelope horns.

More than 15,000 drawings and engravings make up the Tassali rock art.

Samburu women dance and sing during a traditional ceremony.

The ancient Tassili rock paintings seem to be early versions of African clothing with a spiritual message or shamanistic meaning that is still in effect today. Some well-known images that have been mistakenly identified as "aliens" are similar to masks worn by current African cultures that express spiritual power. Others are a close match for woven raffia costumes from Mali and other African nations that cover the entire body and head of a shaman or chieftain.

African ceremonial clothing is diverse, with some traditions incorporating Western cloth-like velvet or Eastern cloth such as silk. Some of today's traditions date back to the rock art of the Tassili people, as can be seen from the paintings and incised rock images that have survived in the dry Sahara climate for thousands of years.

African Cloth Made out of Tree Bark, from Ancient Times to Today

In most parts of Africa, clothing wasn't needed for warmth, but it was needed for protection of other types, including from rain or during battles. African bark cloth dates to the Stone Age and was made by peeling bark from trees and pounding it until it was soft. Vegetable or bark dyes provided patterns and decoration. Similar cloth was also made by ancient Polynesians.

THE CAFTAN

The caftan (or kaftan) is considered the national dress of Morocco in North Africa. It is worn by men and women throughout Africa today, but its origins are in ancient Persia in the Middle East.

A caftan is a long-sleeved, floor-length dress or sheath that may have a simple round or more detailed jeweled or cut-out neckline. Most caftans are loose and flowing and made from cool, comfortable fabrics. In Mali, Nigeria, and other parts of West and Central Africa, the caftan is called a *boubou*. Men wear *boubous* and women wear *m'boubous*. Olusegun Obasanjo, the former president of Nigeria, is noted for his luxurious *boubous*, mostly made from silk. Men wear the *boubou* over narrow trousers and a long-sleeved shirt. Women's *m'boubous* are flowing gowns worn on top of body-wrapping fabric. Headdresses are almost always worn with *m'boubous*. The *agbada* is a Nigerian version of a *boubou* that is an embroidered gown with long, wide sleeves. Some *agbadas* have short sleeves and are made of very lightweight, free-flowing fabric.

In parts of West and Central Africa, men wear a boubou.

ADIRE WITH INDIGO

Adire is a fabric dyeing technique created by the Yoruba in southern Nigeria. *Adire* is a word combining *adi* and *re*, meaning "to dye." The primary dye for *adire* is indigo, known to most people in the United States as the color of blue jeans. *Adire eleko* fabric patterns are intricate geometric designs that sometimes resembled quilts. The patterns are made by painting the designs on fabric with cassava paste and then immersing the fabric in indigo dye.

The oldest traditional *adire* technique is *adire oniko*. Artists tie the fabric with raffia ties and immerse it in indigo dye. When the ties are removed, intricate patterns emerge. Tie-dyeing has been practiced around the world for centuries—it's considered the oldest way of creating a pattern through dye, rather than weaving. *Adire alabere* takes the raffia resist process one step further. Strips of raffia are sewn into the fabric before immersion in dye. When the strips are removed, intricate lines and patterns emerge.

A woman wears adire *clothing.*

ANKARA FABRIC'S BRILLIANT PATTERNS

Ankara fabric is also called Dutch wax fabric. As its name suggests, Ankara fabric wasn't originally made in Africa. It originated in Indonesia and was a Dutch imitation of traditional Indonesian batik wax print fabrics, using block prints. Indonesians didn't want the fabric because it competed with their own local batik industry. First introduced in what was then called the "Gold Coast" (today's Ghana), Ankara fabric became popular in West Africa. In the 1920s, additional designs increased Ankara fabric's popularity, including fabric with portraits of African leaders.

The same concept of brightly colored fabrics with intricate patterns continues in today's Ankara fabric, which can be printed on any underlying fabric from spandex to silk. Most often, the fabric is printed on smooth cotton with detailed, brilliantly colored designs. Today, Ankara fabric is manufactured all over the world. Increasingly, it is imported to Africa from China.

Ankara fabrics are brightly colored with intricate patterns.

MADIBA PRESIDENTIAL SHIRTS

Nelson Mandela sat with Australia's Governor-General in 2009 wearing one of his famous Madiba shirts.

Sometimes associated with the *dashiki*, the Madiba shirt is a contemporary African style that was made popular by legendary South African President Nelson Mandela. When Mandela was elected president in South Africa's first full election in 1994, the designer Desre Buirski gave him a gift of a hand-printed shirt with big gold fish swimming on it—known as the "Big Fish" shirt today.

Mr. Mandela loved the shirt and requested more in different patterns for international appearances and important occasions. Buirski named the shirts Madiba, which is Nelson Mandela's Xhosa clan name. The shirts have a relaxed, elegant fit with Ankara cloth dyed designs integrated with the construction, including the collar, sleeves, and buttons.

NIGERIAN DESIGNER LISA FOLAWIYO

Lisa Folawiyo is a globally successful womenswear and accessory designer from Nigeria who has been featured in *Vogue, Harper's Bazaar, Essence, and Marie Claire.* Her designs began with embellishing Ankara cloth with textures. Her early collections included jeweled and embellished details. She styled long and short dresses with European tailoring but with African prints, colors, and fabrics. As her designs have evolved, she has mixed African silhouettes and draping styles with the tailored skirts and blouses of her early collections. Folawiyo won the African Fashion Awards in 2012. She was originally trained as a lawyer and founded her company in Nigeria in 2005.

Lisa Folawiyo's designs are heavily influenced by Ankara cloth. She embellishes this cloth with textures and jewels.

SOUTH AFRICAN KNITWEAR DESIGNER LADUMA NGXOKOLO

Vivid Xhosa colors, patterns, and story-telling are evident in menswear collections by the South African knitwear designer Laduma Ngxokolo. Laduma's brand, Maxhosa, began with his desire to create contemporary, comfortable knitwear for men who were being initiated in traditional Xhosa rituals. He sought to duplicate Xhosa beadwork with South African wool and mohair (silky hair from an Angora goat). Laduma's other collections include knits inspired by his mother, who taught him to machine-knit when he was 16, and a nostalgic collection called "Buyele'mbo," inspired by the rural lifestyle in the Xhosa homeland in South Africa.

South African Knitwear designer Laduma Ngxokolo sought to duplicate Xhosa beadwork with South African wool and mohair (silky hair from an Angora goat) for his menswear collection.

IKIRÉ JONES BLENDS THE WEST AND AFRICA

Ikiré Jones is the design label of Walé Oyéjidé, the creative director and designer, and Samuel Hubler, the head tailor. Oyéjidé's fabric designs combine the art of the Renaissance with African colors and themes. With the motto "Clothing for a Higher Calling," Ikiré Jones's clothing blends history, culture, and social consciousness in tailored menswear. The designs are unique, with the hallmark of elaborate artistic prints blending European artwork of prior centuries with bold, rich colors and tailoring reflecting the Africa of today.

Designer Walé Oyéjidé looks through pocket squares he designed for his Ikiré Jones line.

CHAPTER 2 ASIA

The oldest known pants, discovered in a grave in western China, date back 5,000 years. The trousers were designed for horseback riding and feature a reinforced crotch, narrow legs, and woven strips of patterned details at the knees. Asia is the birthplace of silk and one of the locations where woven cotton originated, and it has one of the most diverse and rich fashion histories on the planet.

SILK: THE ROYAL FABRIC

Silk is an ancient fabric woven from natural protein fibers made by the mulberry silkworm. Silkworms aren't actually worms—they are moth larvae that spin cocoons around themselves from silk fibers. According to the legendary Chinese philosopher Confucius, in about 3000 BCE, Lady Xi Lingshi, the wife of China's first emperor, was having tea under a mulberry tree when a silkworm cocoon fell into her cup. She unraveled the cocoon and realized that cloth could be made from the fibers. Confucius credits Lady Xi Lingshi with teaching people how to raise silkworms and how to use a loom to weave the silk from their cocoons. In reality, archaeologists have discovered silk thread, spinning tools, and fabric dating back between 6,000 and 7,000 years.

The Bible, ancient Roman historians, and Egyptologists mention the use of silk throughout the ancient world, from flowing tunics worn by Roman women to a see-through dress worn by Cleopatra. The ancient Persians unraveled Chinese silk fabric and rewove it into designs that more closely met their taste. When he

A factory worker operates a silk machine.

Silk factory workers work together to create the smoothest textile.

conquered ancient Persia, Alexander the Great demanded a huge tribute of silk after seeing the luxurious fabric.

The formal name for silk production, from silkworm to finished garment, is *sericulture*. Silk was a coveted fabric and major source of Chinese trade in ancient times, and the Chinese zealously guarded the secret of its manufacture. Anyone who revealed the secrets involved in raising silkworms and producing silk fabric could be punished by death. As a result, the ability to make silk was largely unknown outside of Asia until the sixth century, when Byzantine Emperor Justinian sent spies to China and they brought back silkworm eggs hidden in their walking sticks, starting Middle Eastern silk production and trade.

In ancient China, silk clothing was one of the ultimate status symbols. Only royalty were permitted to wear silk, and commoners caught wearing it could be punished. Silk fabric is soft, light, and strong. Its fibers can be dyed any color, and it can also be painted in highly detailed designs.

JAPANESE FASHION: KIMONO TO HARAJUKU

Many people associate the kimono with Japanese clothing, and in fact, that is the original meaning of the word *kimono*: it just meant "clothes." Early Japanese clothes included trousers, skirts, and shirts worn by men and women. During the Heian Period, from 794 to 1185 CE, clothing makers developed a method for cutting fabric and sewing it together in straight lines. The result was a garment that any wearer could fit to the shape of his or her body and could layer to adjust to different climate conditions and seasons.

The Heian Period was Japan's medieval period. During this time Japanese nobility differentiated themselves from common people by wearing the *juni-hitoe*, a long-sleeved, 12-layered kimono that changed with the seasons. Common people in Heian times wore the *kosode*, a short-sleeved kimono with less elaborate layering and narrow, cylindrical sleeves.

A group of women pose for a photo wearing traditional and colorful kimonos.

In addition to its eccentric style, every Sunday, Harajuku takes part in dressing up in their favorite character's costumes.

Japan entered a time of war during the Kamakura and Muromachi Periods, between 1185 and 1573 CE, also known as the time of the shoguns, ruling warlords who employed professional soldiers—men we know as samurai. The clothing of noble men and women became more elaborate during this time, whereas samurai wore *hitatare*, a type of standard under-armor wear. *Hitatare* consisted of a kimono-style jacket and combination of skirt and trouser. Following *hitatare*, the *kataginu* introduced separate layers, with a flowing layered kimono and a stiff overjacket with exaggerated shoulders. Japanese Noh dramas preserve the clothing and manners of medieval Japan, in some cases literally. Some clothing and Noh masks date to their original use in the fourteenth century.

Japanese people today may wear Western clothes, but always with an unmistakable Japanese flair. In Tokyo, Japanese street fashion originates in the neighborhood called Harajuku, but Osaka and other parts of Tokyo also originate youth fashion trends. Harajuku fashions influence designers around the globe, from Louis Vuitton to Marc Jacobs.

SOUTH ASIA'S BRILLIANT COLORS

One of the earliest sculptures from the Indian subcontinent is the famous *Dancing Girl* found in the ancient city of Mohenjo-Daro in Pakistan. The *Dancing Girl* wears only jewelry and no other clothing. It's unlikely that ancient people in Pakistan or India wore no clothes. Men probably wore an early form of *dhoti*, a piece of cloth wrapped around the legs and tied at the waist, forming loose short or long pants. Women probably wore short skirts tied around their waist. Both genders wore head coverings to keep the hot sun from their heads. India is the birthplace of cotton, and examples of woven Indian cotton cloth have been found dating back 5,000 years.

Men in India wear dhoti, kurta, and a turban on their heads.

There is a tradition in the Hindu religion to bathe in the Ganges River. The tradition shows just how colorful the traditional Hindu clothing is.

Present-day traditional clothing in India and Pakistan developed further in the Vedic Period, from 1500 BCE to 500 CE. The Vedic Period is named for the Vedas, legendary stories that are part of the foundation of Hindu culture. Art of the period shows that women wore fitted short-sleeved shirts called *cholis* and skirts tied around their waist. The sari, a traditional Indian women's dress still worn today, was invented during the Vedic Period. The sari is a long single piece of cloth that is draped about the body.

Men in the Vedic period first wore *dhotis* without a shirt, but the *kurta*, a loose-fitting shirt, eventually became fashionable. Loose-fitting pajama pants emerged during the Vedic Period, as did the turban formed from long strips of cloth wrapped around the head. Colors have been important throughout Indian history for both men's and women's clothing. Some cultural differences may surprise Westerners, however. White is the color of funerals, for example, and only widows are traditionally allowed to wear white. Red stands for purity as well as the fiery Hindu goddess Durga; it is preferred as a bridal color.

Brilliant colors in endless variety are synonymous with Indian clothing and fashion. The Hindu festival of Holi celebrates the arrival of spring, fertility, the triumph of good over evil, and the endless variety of colors.

THE SIMPLE, VERSATILE SARONG

The sarong is a traditional piece of clothing made from a single piece of fabric that is tied around the body and worn throughout Southeast Asia, Africa, and the Middle East. *Sarong* simply means "covering" in Malay. Sarongs are usually made from soft woven cotton dyed using batik, an Indonesian wax-resistance dyeing technique. Other popular sarong fabrics include plaid or checked patterns, particularly among men.

Sarongs can be tied in dozens of ways, but they are most commonly tied around the waist or at the shoulder. In some countries, like Sri Lanka, only men wear a sarong, and they wear it only to mosques on Sundays. The sarong has been adopted throughout Polynesia, where it's called a *pareu* or *lavalava*. In Java, men often wear sarongs and embroidered shirts or lightweight jackets. In South Asia, including Bangladesh, India, and Pakistan, sarongs are slightly different from *dhotis*, which are worn as pants. Called a *lungi* in Bangladesh, men and boys wear sarongs more as wraparound skirts than as trousers.

Men wear traditional sarongs as they wait to take the stage and dance.

Indian workers make soft coverlets from natural cotton in front of a small workshop.

COTTON AND INDIA

The first evidence of cotton in the Eastern Hemisphere dates from 6000 BCE, including thread and cloth fragments found in the Indus delta in present-day Pakistan. Cotton itself is native to nearly every continent, and evidence of early cotton-growing and weaving has also been found in South America.

Cotton fibers are primarily cellulose, and the fibers can easily be spun and woven into cloth. Between 3300 and 1300 BCE, the cotton industry became well developed in India. Indian cotton fabric was the largest export of India's legendary Mughal Empire, which existed between the sixteenth and eighteenth centuries. A cotton gin, a machine that mechanically separates cotton fibers from its seeds, was invented in India in the thirteenth century, coming into wide use during the Mughal era. This era of cotton fabric production fueled the vast, wealthy Mughal Empire and continues to be influential today in the infinite variety of textures, colors, and weaves of cotton made in India.

THE SIKH TURBAN

The turban is a tightly wrapped head covering that typically allows no underlying hair to be visible. The turban is most closely associated with Sikh people from the Punjab region in northern India. The Sikh religion emerged during the fifteenth century—the word *sikh* means "disciple." For Sikhs, the turban is more than a head covering or fashion statement; it is part of their religion.

Sikh males do not cut their hair and wear a turban on their heads. It can be wrapped in different shapes, as seen here.

The Sikh turban also has an origin in Sikhism's belief in equality. When their religion was forming in the medieval era, only the wealthiest elites in Punjab wore turbans. Sikhs began wearing turbans as a way to indicate their social equality. Sikh men and women alike do not cut their hair. The Sikh turban covers long hair, which both men and women keep in a bun underneath their head covering. Turbans may be prewrapped or may be made of different lengths of fabric, which are wrapped in different styles to create rounder or more angular shapes.

Both men and women wear hanboks in Korea.

KOREAN HANBOK: UNUSUAL SILHOUETTES

Hanbok means "Korean clothing." The *hanbok* is traditional wear for Korean men and women. The style of *hanbok* for both genders represents a silhouette that is unusual in Western and Eastern clothing traditions. Both men and women wear a short jacket called a *jeogori*. Mens' *jeogoris* are waist-length, whereas Western eyes would call women's *jeogoris* "crop tops." Women wear long, full skirts called *chimas* that begin at the chest, while men wear loose-fitting trousers called *bajis*. *Hanboks* were on display during the 2018 Seoul Winter Olympics.

Hanboks were relegated to formalwear in Korea for decades, but contemporary versions are becoming more popular on Korean streets. Modern Korean *hanbok* designers include Dew Hwang, who makes contemporary *hanboks* for everyday wear. Western designers such as Karl Lagerfeld have featured *hanboks* in Eastern-inspired design collections.

JAPANESE YOUTH FASHION

Tokyo has entire districts devoted to youth fashion, in addition to the world-famous Harajuku (now called Ura-Harajuku). Japanese youth who are part of fashion culture are estimated to participate actively for about four years. Japanese youth fashion is influenced by pop culture, and it also influences pop culture. Styles include ultra-feminine Lolita, which are saccharine-sweet ruffles, and parasols to dark, grungy, girly goth. *Kei* for both men and women is somewhat inspired by Western glam rock but with a unique Japanese twist. Japanese youth fashion is ever-changing and extreme and is a major international street fashion influence.

These girls are wearing pink Lolita-style outfits and makeup in Harajuku.

Models sporting Issey Miyake's designs at Paris Fashion Week.

ISSEY MIYAKE, FASHION LEGEND

Issey Miyake was born before the Second World War in Hiroshima, Japan, and he has become one of the world's most famous fashion designers. In the 1960s he designed for Givenchy before moving to Geoffrey Beene. In 1970 Miyake began his own design studio. His fashions are known for innovative materials, construction (including revolutionary pleating techniques), and elegant simplicity. Techies may recognize fashion through Miyake because he designed the signature black turtlenecks worn by Apple's Steve Jobs. He is also known for his blending of technology and fashion, and he was a pioneer in designer fragrances with his signature scent, L'eau d'Issey.

LAKMÉ FASHION WEEK

Lakmé Fashion Week takes place twice a year in Mumbai, India. Since its inception in 1999, Lakmé Fashion Week has become increasingly influential, and it now has millions of fans on social media as well as global media coverage. The event sponsor, Lakmé, is India's top cosmetic and

Models showcase designs from Soumitra Mondal Marg at Lakmé Fashion Week.

salon company. With both summer/resort and winter/festive events held each year, auditions for the week are open and highly competitive among Indian designers. Fashion artists from all over India are featured at the show and include men's, women's, traditional, and avant-garde fashions.

ICONIC MADRAS PLAID

Madras was formerly the name of India's city of Chennai, and Madras plaid is the name for cotton fabric that was historically made in that city and initially exported around the world by the East India Company. Originally a simple fabric for poor Indians, Madras plaid is woven from cotton yarn dyed by hand and should appear the same on inner and exterior sides. Today, authentic Madras plaid is made by descendants of 400 original weaving families in more than 200 villages in the region. Madras plaid shirts, shorts, and blindingly loud golf pants have been a status symbol in the United States off and on since the 1930s.

Madras plaid originated in India, but over the years it has made its way into other countries and cultures. Pictured here, Natalie Portman wears a Madras dress at a U.S. Open Tournament.

CHAPTER **3** EUROPE

Signs of ancient clothing in Europe could possibly date back 170,000 years, and archaeologists have found evidence of Neanderthal clothing dating back 60,000 years. Ancient Greeks and Romans focused on hairstyles and fabrics to denote wealth and status, whereas the earliest signs of an emerging fashion culture in Europe date to the Middle Ages. Europe is also home to the first modern fashion design house: the nineteenth-century House of Worth.

GREEKS AND ROMANS WORE MORE THAN TOGAS

Recent archaeological discoveries have added to the information that clothing historians knew about Greek and Roman clothing from surviving stone and bronze statues. In both ancient Greece and Rome, statues depicted gods, goddesses, and rulers, so their clothing represents ideal garments worn by elites. Traditional garments such as togas, tunics, and *chitons* required belts to fit both men and women. Women wore their tunics belted beneath the breasts, and men belted their tunics around the waist or hips.

Sculptures of Greek gods, goddesses, rulers, and philosophers often show the men and women draped in tunics.

Ancient Greeks and Romans wore vibrant colors, not exclusively white clothing, as was often assumed. Scientists have revealed that marble statues, which were assumed for generations to be pure white, were in fact originally painted in brilliant colors. A reconstruction of the statue of a kneeling archer from the Temple of Aphaia (or Afea) on the Greek island of Aegina features a rainbow of colors and intricate patterns on the archer's tunic, pants, and sleeves. The archer's pants are so formfitting that they must represent something made from knitted fabric. Ancient Greeks and Romans

This mosaic portrays what female Roman athletes wore while competing in Olympic-inspired sports.

fashioned socks, caps, and gloves in this manner. Men and women primarily wore sandals, and in cold weather they added warmth with socks.

A famous mosaic found in a Sicilian villa shows 10 female Roman athletes competing in Olympic-inspired sports wearing brown two-piece bikinis. The bikinis were likely made from soft leather, similar to the leather underwear worn by a Roman cavalry soldier that has been discovered. In addition to leather, the Romans used wool, cotton, and silk for clothing. Exotic fabrics and dyes were imported from India, China, and other parts of the Mediterranean.

It's extremely unlikely that togas were everyday wear, even for the highest ranking Roman men. A single piece of toga-wrapping fabric could be up to 20 feet (6 meters) long. Slaves had to help noble Romans don their togas, and once on, the men had to carry the excess fabric draped over one arm all day. Robes, scarves, hats, veils, headbands, head wraps, and shift dresses all have their roots in ancient Roman styles.

MEDIEVAL EUROPE: THE AGE OF LUXURY

Medieval Europe was a more stylish and luxurious place than ragged peasants dressed in tunics and traveling priests in brown wool cassocks with a rope tied around their waist. This was a time and place of expanding boundaries and trade, with elaborate weaving techniques producing brocades using silk thread from China and the exploitation of many types of animal fur for cloaks and lining.

The middle class grew in Europe during the medieval period, from the tenth to fifteenth centuries, and even poorer people gained the resources to buy more elaborate clothing than the tunics and sandals worn during Roman times. Clothing became associated with class and status—in minute detail of color, fabric, and style—resulting in "sumptuary laws." With a name derived from the word *sumptuous* (meaning expensive and luxurious), sumptuary laws defined what fabrics could be worn by the wealthy, the middle class, and the poor. The laws didn't stop there, though: They even specified the length of toes on boots for knights or squires and how much money women could spend on veils, depending on their social status.

Fabrics and materials that are still associated with luxury were well known in medieval Europe, including fur and velvet. Velvet made from silk threads had been

Not all people lived lavishly in medieval Europe. Many lived in the middle class and wore muted colors, fabrics, and styles in comparison to those who were wealthier.

Women in medieval Europe look similar to how we depict Disney princesses.

made in China for hundreds of years, and Italian cities began making velvet in the twelfth century. Medieval velvet took countless hours to weave and often included gold and silver threads within the soft cut pile that creates velvet's unique texture.

The look we associate with Disney princesses also originated in medieval Europe. Cone-shaped "princess hats," called *hennins*, were based on tall felt hats called *boqtas*, worn by Mongolian warrior queens. According to legend, Marco Polo brought a *boqta* back from China, and the fashion style was born. Other extreme medieval fashions included long pointed sleeves for men and women, extensive trains up to 32 feet (10 m) long on gowns and cloaks, and pointed slippers made from silk brocade, gold, and silver. Fashionable men and women began wearing clogs and heeled shoes to increase their height—another innovation brought to Europe from Asia along the legendary Silk Road.

The World's Oldest Socks

The oldest known pair of socks were made with a split-toe Greek style and were found preserved in the Egyptian desert. The socks still retain their red color and are formfitting, knitted with a time-consuming single-needle technique.

PARIS: FASHION CAPITAL OF THE WORLD

Paris's reputation as a fashion capital originated in the seventeenth-century reign of the renowned "Sun King," Louis XIV, who also created the stunning gardens and palace of Versailles. The Sun King took control of many arts and crafts industries, including textile making and clothing design. Louis was the final arbiter of French and European style, and his taste was lavish, defining the art, decor, and fashion period known as the Baroque. Parisian tastes continued to lead fashion in Europe until the nineteenth century, when the centuries-old craft of tailors and seamstresses evolved into haute couture.

Haute couture is luxury fashion made specifically for wealthy and stylish patrons. Clothiers, seamstresses, and tailors had created clothes for patrons in Europe for centuries, but in 1858 Charles Frederick Worth coined the term "fashion designer" and opened the first great fashion house in Paris. The emphasis changed from clothing that expressed the wealth of patrons to the designer's artistry and taste. Ten years later, the Chambre Syndicale de la Haute Couture was established to safeguard the quality of Parisian high fashion. By 1948, Paris was home to more than 100 certified couture fashion houses.

Models showcase designer Karl Lagerfeld's Chanel haute couture line at Paris Fashion Week.

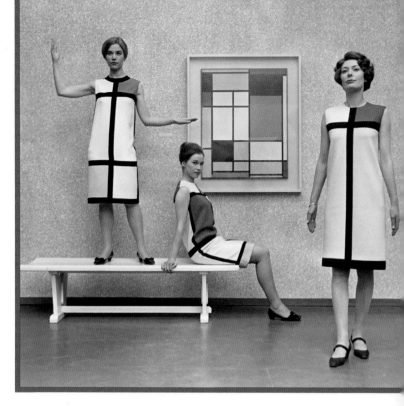

In the twentieth century, major fashion houses like Dior and Chanel released collections that began to define Paris as a world style leader. Coco Chanel not only became the first world-famous female fashion designer, she also changed women's clothing forever by eliminating painful and restricting corsets. Chanel jackets, the "little black dress," and beautiful flapper dresses defined some of the most important looks in early twentieth-

Yves Saint Laurent Mondrian collection circa 1965.

century women's fashion. Givenchy and Balmain continued the world influence of Parisian fashion.

When Yves Saint Laurent opened his boutique Saint Laurent Rive Gauche in 1966, fashion boutiques and Parisian ready-to-wear clothing (*prêt-à-porter*) began to influence apparel worn by women around the world. Other influential 1960s Parisian designers include Pierre Cardin, André Courrèges, and Emanuel Ungaro.

Today, Paris remains a world fashion capital, but it shares the title with Milan, New York, and London. Fashion weeks in each city launch seasonal collections by the world's greatest designers and influence what men and women wear around the world.

What Is "Royal Purple"?

The famous, valuable royal Tyrian purple color was a vivid, deep red-purple made from murex shells, a type of sea snail. Even the noblest Romans sometimes preferred cheaper substitute colors, because dye makers boiled the snails for days in lead pots, producing a foul odor that made finished garments smell like rotten fish.

HOUSE OF CHANEL

Coco Chanel was one of the earliest (and remains one of the most successful) female entrepreneurs in European history. Born in 1883, Chanel is the only fashion designer on *Time* magazine's list of Most Influential People in the twentieth century. Chanel deconstructed women's restrictive, formal nineteenth-century fashions and created casual, comfortable, and chic clothing using knit jersey fabric that women loved and found flattering and easy to wear. Chanel created her own Double-C logo and was responsible for originating Chanel No. 5, which remains one of the world's most loved and recognized fragrances. She created the Chanel suit, the Chanel bag, and the famous "little black dress."

Chanel's memory is sadly marred by her involvement with Nazis during the Parisian occupation in the Second World War. Her life has inspired Broadway musicals and several films.

Models take the runway at the Chanel show. The company's style is very much influenced by the company's founder, Coco.

Department stores are filled with ready-to-wear displays like the one pictured here.

PRÊT-À-PORTER, OR
READY-TO-WEAR

The Industrial Revolution created massive changes in how clothes were made and worn. Up until the early part of the twentieth century, clothes were mostly made for individuals. Women sewed the clothing for their family, whereas people with better financial means could afford tailors and seamstresses, who made individual items of clothing one at a time.

The concept of *prêt-à-porter*, or ready-to-wear, dates to the Victorian era. Clothing was mass-produced in factories that often employed child labor. Large department stores emerged in the late nineteenth century, presenting clothing styles to the general public. Knock-off imitations of high-fashion clothing entered department stores as soon as they opened. The development of standard sizing during the late 1930s and 1940s increased the ability of manufacturers to mass-produce and sell clothing. Today, the world fashion industry is seasonal, and nearly all fashion houses sell ready-to-wear collections in boutiques and department stores around the world.

ITALIAN FASHION EQUALS LUXURY

During the first part of the twentieth century, Italian fashion was somewhat eclipsed by Parisian superstar fashion designers like Chanel and Dior. But Italy has been a cradle of luxury and craftsmanship since Roman times and the Renaissance. Italy's twentieth-century fashion renaissance began in the 1950s with Gucci and Ferragamo, both producing clothing and accessories synonymous with quality and glamor.

In 2009 and 2014, Milan was ranked as the world's top fashion capital, and it frequently alternates in the top four rankings with London, New York, and Paris. Italian designers are often associated with high levels of craftsmanship and luxury in apparel and accessories. Italian clothing designers also focus on menswear and womenswear, particularly houses like Armani and Fendi. Missoni, Valentino, Versace, Prada, and Dolce & Gabbana are headquartered in Milan, and each helms a lifestyle brand that encompasses haute couture, streetwear and sportswear, fragrances, and accessories.

Founded by Gianni Versace in 1978, the luxury clothing line continues to be one of the top brands in Europe and the world.

BEAU BRUMMEL, "THE DANDY"

Men's fashion magazines like *GQ* owe their commitment to tailoring, fit, and style in menswear to the original "dandy," an eighteenth-century British nobleman named George "Beau" Brummell. Brummell was the first arbiter of men's fashion and taste in Europe, partly owing to his close friendship with the Prince Regent, who would become King George IV. His name is still associated with style, taste, and quality. Brummell did away with elaborate formalwear—powdered wigs, makeup, and knee-length breeches—for men and introduced full-length trousers, fitted coats, and white shirts and cravats (an early necktie) made from fine linen. Brummel was known for his charm and wit as well as his elegant manner of dress, but one day he went too far and, referring to the Prince Regent, asked, "Who's your fat friend?" He quickly fell from favor, and died in poverty in France.

This caricature depicts Beau Brummel and his style in 1805.

WHEN DID WOMEN START WEARING PANTS?

Coco Chanel was one of the pioneers of women's pants, a trend that would have been considered impossible in Europe any time before the twentieth century. Ancient Greek vases show Amazon women wearing short tunics and long, straight pants, but the style was associated only with warriors. In the early part of the twentieth century, the introduction of bicycles inspired clothing makers to design pants for bicycle riding. More styles were added for tennis, horseback riding, and hunting. By the 1930s, many film stars were wearing pants on screen. In the 1940s, World War II introduced pants to nearly every woman's wardrobe, as women went to work in factories wearing their husband's work clothes while the husbands went off to war.

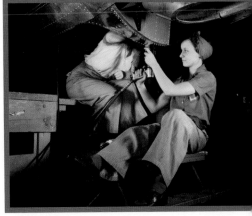

During World War II, women were called to work in factories while the men were fighting. They began wearing their husbands' clothing rather than their normal dresses or skirts.

BUSTLES AND FARTHINGALES

During the early Renaissance, most European women wore flowing gowns without interior structure. As clothing became more elaborate, women's dresses and undergarments began to take on the characteristics of an engineering project, meant to exaggerate desirable features. Farthingales were structured hoop skirts that originated in Spain. Hoops made of whalebone supported bell-like skirts that eventually reached massive proportions by the 1590s, as illustrated in a portrait of Elizabeth I by Sir Henry Lee of Ditchley. A bustle was a similar undergarment dating from the nineteenth century that lifted the back of a woman's skirt, creating a shelf-like silhouette and preventing skirt hems from dragging on the ground.

Women wore farthingales throughout the late 1500s.

On his wedding day, Prince Harry wore a formal frock coat.

SAVILE ROW

If you've heard the word *bespoke*, which means tailored perfectly for one person, it is synonymous with the London street Savile Row. Located in Mayfair, in the middle of London, Savile Row tailoring is legendary for its fit and craftsmanship. Suits made precisely to the measurements of customers are the hallmark of the row of tailors that originated in 1846 with the opening of Henry Poole & Co. at number 32 Savile Row. Both men and women wear bespoke clothing from Savile Row. In 2018, Prince William and Prince Harry wore formal frock coats made by Dege & Skinner for the royal wedding of Harry and Meghan Markle.

CHAPTER 4 LATIN AMERICA AND THE CARIBBEAN

Some of the world's most famous and successful fashion designers come from Latin America, including Carolina Herrera and Oscar de la Renta. Clothing and fashion in the Caribbean and Latin America is diverse and influenced by pre-Columbian cultures like the Maya, Aztec, and Inca, as well as the dramatic, multicultural history of the Caribbean.

EARLY CENTRAL AMERICAN CLOTHING

Traditional dress in Central America, also called *traje* (tra-heh), echoes the days of the Maya and Aztec empires. The *huipil* is worn throughout the region (also called Mesoamerica) and is a direct descendant of clothing worn by Maya and Aztec women. A short or long tunic with a square neck and short sleeves, the *huipil* is made from two rectangular sections of fabric. The sections are joined together with stitching or ribbons.

One of the most famous *huipils* is "La Malinche," an off-white tunic embroidered with gold thread and decorated with feathers, now housed in Mexico's National Museum of Anthropology. The garment is named after Hernan Cortez's translator, although she didn't wear it—it has been dated to 100 years after her lifetime. Other forms of traditional clothing, from shawls to hats, sandals, dresses, and trousers, continue to be worn throughout the region.

A woman weaves a traditional huipil *at the loom.*

Mayan dancers continue to wear traditional clothing when they dance in honor of their culture and their ancestors.

Today, about 42 million people live in Central America (Belize, Costa Rica, El Salvador, Guatemala, Honduras, Nicaragua, and Panama). In addition to carved stele that represent ceremonial clothing worn by Mayan nobility, frescos, ceramics, and books called *codices* survive and give a picture of how exotic ancient Mayan clothing was.

Dance is still an important part of Central American culture, and in precolonial times, Mayan dancers wore extravagant beaded and feathered costumes that included large headdresses decorated with brilliant feathers and back racks trailing feathered stripes. Men entering battle or participating in ceremonies wore animal hides and feathers indicating their spiritual power, particularly jaguar hides. Men and women wore nose and ear jewelry made from jade, ceramics, and gold.

The ancient Maya created elaborate clothing that showed social status and indicated spiritual or physical prowess. In addition to using brightly colored bird feathers, the Maya used natural colors like indigo, sea shell purple, and cochineal red to dye natural plant fibers and cotton, which they wove into complex designs on a backstrap loom. This loom is still used today to create woven panels for *huipils* and other traditional clothing. Cotton evolved independently in the Americas and has been used for thousands of years. Mayan *codices* show rolls and stacks of folded cloth used as tribute, and inscriptions illustrate the elaborate, hand crafted clothing, and the jade and gold jewelry and headpieces worn at the height of the Mayan Empire.

SOUTH AMERICAN CLOTHING

The two main ways of creating clothing through history are weaving and tailoring. Clothing that is created either wholly or partially on a loom is made by weaving. Tailoring involves cutting pattern pieces out of already woven fabric and joining them. Most ancient people around the world used both techniques, but some preferred one strategy over the other, depending on climate and taste. In South America, the majority of clothing was woven on a loom, sometimes in a single piece. One of the main achievements of South American clothing, particularly in the Andes, is elaborate woven designs and garments.

The Inca are the best known civilization of coastal and mountain South America, but they're not the only civilization to thrive in the region. The Chimú people created the large city of Chan Chan and wove spectacular illustrated tapestries that were worn as shirts, tunics, or floor-length gowns. The Chimú also made elaborate, beautiful gold jewelry worn by leaders and religious figures. Based on drawings and ceramics, the Moche people were masters of graphic design, with bold spirals and bands of dark and light color decorating shields, tunics, and their faces and bodies. The Moche were warlike, and many of their textiles and costumes depict fierce gods with sharp fangs, including one recurring figure that anthropologists call "The Decapitator."

In South America, looms are still used to create elaborate woven designs and garments.

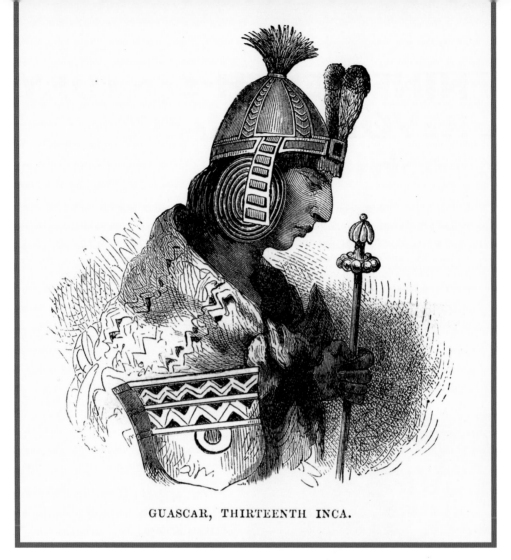

GUASCAR, THIRTEENTH INCA.

Inca's Sapa Inca wore ceremonial cloaks made from bird feathers, gold, and precious gems.

Clothing marked status in the Inca Empire, up to and including the Inca ruler, Sapa Inca. Like some of today's high-status fashion addicts, Sapa Inca wore everyday clothing only once. He wore a ceremonial cloak made from scarlet bird feathers, gold, and precious gems. From commoner to Sapa Inca, most people wore tunics made from a large square piece of woven cloth. Men and women alike fastened open portions of the tunic with copper, gold, or silver pins. Inca people used a wide range of vegetable and animal dyes to create vibrant colors. They used cotton for most clothing, but they wove warm clothes for cold mountain weather made from llama, alpaca, or vicuña wool. Vicuña wool is extremely soft, and the finest Inca textiles had a thread count rivaling today's softest luxury woven fabric.

NINETEENTH-CENTURY REVOLUTIONARY FASHION

South America was primarily colonized by the Spanish, with the exception of Brazil, which was colonized by Portugal. The Dutch colonized Suriname and the Caribbean islands of Aruba and Dutch Antilles. Each area had its own native culture that the colonial nations sought to suppress during the colonial era, which lasted from Columbus's voyage in 1492 to 1832. This period is the reason why North and South American cultures prior to 1492 are called "pre-Columbian."

Revolutions in the United States and France, along with a growing desire for freedom, inspired South American movements for independence. Simón Bolívar led a 10-year battle for Venezuela's independence from Spain between 1808 and 1919. He eventually became the leader of a union of several independent South American nations called Gran Colombia. Bolívar not only created a political revolution, he also initiated revolutionary fashions, including designing his own uniforms with South American colors, styling, and insignia. The liberator of Argentina, José de San Martín, also followed an independent path in designing his own clothing and military uniforms.

Like Napoleon, who established a new era of fashion and design in France following the French Revolution, Bolívar, San Martín, and other revolutionaries created a new mythology for their nations. Women joined in the new era, wearing clothing with influences from pre-Columbian indigenous peoples and changing European fashions to reflect their new national identity. In Argentina, women changed the Spanish hair comb called a *peineta* into a dramatic three-foot *peineton*, echoing the headdresses of previous eras.

Simón Bolívar was revolutionary in South American politics as well as fashion.

This artwork portrays the giant hair combs worn by Argentinian women in the new era.

Early postcolonial regimes in South America sometimes issued strict fashion edicts. In Argentina, the revolutionary leader Juan Manuel de Rosas ordered all men to wear red revolutionary insignia on their vests. The Argentine political opposition wore light blue, and in response, de Rosas banned the color from public wear. An influential public fashion voice, although it only published 23 issues, *La Moda* fashion magazine was founded in Argentina in 1837. The magazine combined fashion with politics, inspired by the Parisian magazine *La Mode*, which served as a style and culture arbiter during the French Revolution. The mixture of European influence with Latin American style established during the early days of postcolonial independence continues throughout the region today.

Amazonian Clothing: Minimal and Influential

In 1541 the Spanish soldier Francisco de Orellana traveled up the Amazon River and encountered fierce female warriors whom he called Amazons, inspired by the mythical female Greek warriors. Indigenous Brazilian people were regarded as "naked savages" by settlers, who today adopt their thongs and tangas as beachwear on Brazil's famous white sand beaches.

CUBA'S FASHION INFLUENCE

The island of Cuba is associated with rum, salsa, revolution, and cigars, and it's also been a fashion trendsetter throughout its history. Spanish and African culture and clothing both play a role in Cuban fashion. The island's tropical climate launched fashion trends necessary to cope with heat and humidity. None of these is more famous than the Cuban shirt, also called a *guayabera*. The *guayabera* is a short-sleeved, lightweight shirt with two rows of sewn pleats and patch pockets. The shirt is worn throughout Central America and Mexico, but it dates back to the 1880s and its name tells the story: Its originator sewed shirts for her husband to carry guavas home from the fields.

Dresses inspired by dances like rumba and salsa originated the elaborate ruffled and off-shoulder dress styles associated with Cuban women's fashion. Head wraps are referred to as bandanas in Cuba, and whether the style is sleek or elaborate, this Afro-Cuban influence is seen on beaches and in tropical climates worldwide. The Cuban version of a Panama hat, a white woven fedora with a dark band, is a classic of midcentury casual men's fashion.

Women's fashion in Cuba is made up of elaborate ruffled dresses and bandanas.

The women of Bolivia often wear bowler hats.

DISTINCTIVE LATIN AMERICAN HATS

The woven, brimmed Panama hat originated not in Panama but in Ecuador. The light-colored hat continues to be woven from palm fibers throughout Central America. Women throughout Central and South America wear hats not just for protection and fashion, but also as a form of identity.

In both Bolivia and Peru, indigenous women wear bowler hats that bear a surprising resemblance to British bowler hats worn by Winston Churchill. The hats arrived in the region in the 1920s, meant for British workers building a railway. The hats that arrived were too small for the male workers, but they fit women's heads perfectly. The fashion trend is now part of daily wear throughout the area, often decorated with brightly colored woven bands and sometimes with fresh flowers. Bolivian women are called *cholitas*, a diminutive of *cholo*—a regular guy or indigenous man in Spanish.

GREAT LADIES' INFLUENCE ON FASHION

Women influence culture and fashion in a uniquely Latin American way, thanks to the combined traditions of Iberian-European culture (Spain and Portugal) and indigenous peoples. Argentina's twentieth-century First Lady Eva Perón, known as Evita, used her status to advance women's rights and conditions for poor Argentinian women and children. Evita was born in a poor village in the Argentine Pampas in 1919. She became an actress, and her beauty and charm attracted the future Argentine leader Juan Perón. She was one of the most fashion-conscious female leaders in the twentieth century and elegantly wore fashions by world designers, including Christian Dior. She employed fashion assistants and sponsored Argentine designers, expanding haute couture in the country and throughout the region.

Argentina is not alone in having a history of political turmoil and assassination, but the country has experienced repeated instances of human rights violations. Between 1976 and 1983, more than 30,000 Argentinians "disappeared" in senseless government-sponsored terror killings. The mothers of the *desaparecidos* (the disappeared) gathered in Argentina's Plaza de Mayo in 1977. The white scarves worn by the Mothers of the Plaza de Mayo symbolized the children they had lost. Their movement continues today throughout the region in support of human rights.

Evita Perón often wore fashions by famous designers such as Christian Dior.

CAROLINA HERRERA

Polished, sophisticated, and personally stylish, Carolina Herrera is one of the world's most famous designers of formal womenswear. She is known for dressing many international leading ladies, including U.S. First Ladies Jacqueline Onassis, Michelle Obama, and Laura Bush. Herrera was born in

Models take the runway in Carolina Herrera's designs at New York Fashion Week.

the Venezuelan capital of Caracas in 1939. She did not initially plan to become a fashion designer, but launched her first collection in 1981 with the encouragement of *Vogue* and *Harper's Bazaar* editor Diana Vreeland. Herrera's designs are known for their timeless elegance and simplicity. CH Carolina Herrera is now a world lifestyle and fashion brand known for upscale womenswear, accessories, and fragrance.

ISABEL TOLEDO

Isabel Toledo, born in Cuba in 1961, is a New York–based designer who has a background in painting, ceramics, and fashion design. She has received numerous awards for her collections, including the Cooper-Hewitt National Design Award. Her designs are sometimes better known to fashion insiders than the general public, but her clothing has been selected as favorites by fashion trendsetters, including Michelle Obama. She partners closely with her husband, Ruben Toledo, who sketches designs while she constructs garments. Isabel Toledo began as a seamstress, and her methods of draping and construction are experimental, based on her deep knowledge of garment construction and fabric.

American actor Debi Mazer wears Isabel Toledo on the red carpet for an event.

CARLOS MIELE

Carlos Miele is often re-garded as Brazil's most famous and successful designer. Based in São Paulo, Miele focuses on women's ready-to-wear under two la-bels: Carlos Miele and Miele. He incorporates traditional Brazilian crafts and tech-

Carlos Miele's designs are often seen at fashion weeks around the world each year.

niques, including leatherwork, patchwork, crochet, and decorative stitching, into his clothing. With a sexy, revealing emphasis, Miele's clothes have been worn by celebrities on the red carpet worldwide. Expressing *amor y sexo* (love and sex-iness), Miele's clothing often includes metallic fabrics, thigh-baring splits, and revealing construction exposing chest, back, and shoulders. His designs reflect the love that Brazilian women have for their bodies and their freedom of expression.

Osacr de la Renta's designs have been worn by leading ladies across America.

OSCAR DE LA RENTA

Oscar de la Renta was born in the Dominican Republic in 1932 and grew up to become one of the world's most renowned fashion designers. First aspir-ing to become a painter, de la Renta moved to Madrid at age 18 to study fine art. His early, clear talent drew the atten-tion of a top Spanish designer, Cristóbal Balenciaga, who made him an apprentice. Balenciaga's refined taste and elegance continued as a theme for de la Renta, and he soon went to work for Lanvin in Paris and Elizabeth

Arden in New York. By 1965 he had established his own fashion house and begun to design the feminine, sophisticated gowns that have been worn by first ladies such as Nancy Reagan, Hillary Clinton, and Laura Bush.

CHAPTER 5 MIDDLE EAST

The Middle East includes Egypt, the Arabian peninsula, Turkey, Iraq, Iran, Lebanon, and Syria; North African countries such as Libya; and countries in western Asia, including Afghanistan. The Middle East is considered the birthplace of human civilization. Influenced by religious revolutions like Islam, fashion in the Middle East today incorporates ancient roots in Persia, Egypt, Israel, and Palestine along with high-tech materials and style.

FASHION IN ANCIENT EGYPT

This 5,000-year-old Tarkhan Dress is thought to be the world's oldest dress.

Modern fashionistas could be tempted to think that all Egyptians went bare-breasted, wore straight white dresses and flat sandals, and stood with both feet facing forward, but the truth is much more diverse. Egypt is one of civilization's birthplaces and home of the Great Pyramids and the Sphinx, monuments that have survived for over 5,000 years. Another ancient survivor is the world's oldest dress. The 5,000-year-old Tarkhan Dress was discovered in an ancient tomb near Cairo in 1913. Its age and importance went unrecognized until the 1970s, when the surprisingly modern-looking V-necked linen garment was dated to between 3482 and 3102 BCE. The dress is preserved and exhibited at the Petrie Museum at University College London, which also houses a stunning 4,000-year-old beaded net dress decorated with silver beads and shells. Egyptians wove fabric from cotton, linen, and wool. Linen is one of the world's oldest fibers, made from the flax plant. Egyptians prized pure white garments and were pioneers of bleaching natural fibers to produce white finished woven textiles, including linen and cotton. During the Fatimid era (969–1171 CE), when Egypt was ruled by an Islamic dynasty, artisans had access to fibers and dyes from around the world, and they wove world-renowned silk fabrics and robes.

Cosmetics, wigs, and fragrances likely didn't originate in ancient Egypt, but Egyptian beauty traditions persist. The ancient bust of Nefertiti shows the sophisticated makeup that Egyptians used to enhance male and female beauty. Egyptians used ground stones like malachite to create blue and green eyeshadow. Kohl, made from the mineral galena, was ground into powder and used to line the eyes for generations. Men and women wore wigs made from human hair that sometimes took elaborate

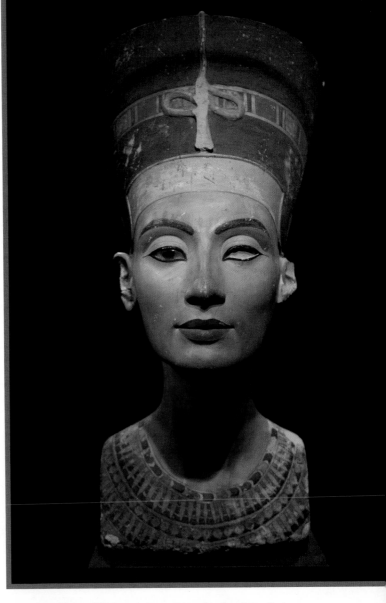

The ancient bust of Nefertiti shows the style of makeup that was used to enhance female beauty. It also shows the type of headdress worn by royalty.

forms. Many types of natural perfume and deodorant were used—and Egyptians invented the toothbrush and toothpaste. Natural herbs mixed with honey served as breath mints. Egyptians believed that the condition of one's body while alive carried into an eternal afterlife, so cosmetics, fragrances, and fashions had both a daily and an eternal purpose.

RELIGION AND ISLAMIC FASHION

Ancient Egyptians related the clothing and fashions they wore in daily life to the way they would look and dress in the afterlife. Thousands of years later, the religion of Islam influences clothing throughout the Middle East. Islamic beliefs include modesty for both men and women. Women are asked to show their beauty within their families and should not wear excessive ornamentation. The Qu'ran instructs Muslim women to cover their head and their breasts with their *khimar*, a type of veil or scarf. The word *hijab* refers to the type of scarf, veil, or covering that provides the modesty prescribed in the Qu'ran.

The hijab varies from nation to nation, and in most countries it is not mandatory for Muslim woman to wear it. Iran is one of the only nations to require a mandatory hijab for women; women in Indonesia's Aceh Province must also wear the hijab while in public. The hijab has taken on more of a cultural and fashion emphasis in other countries, expressing the style of individual Muslim women along with the modesty requested by the Qu'ran. In recent years, Islamic women have created

Middle Eastern women believe in modesty and wear a khimar to cover their head and breasts, in addition to a scarf called a hijab.

modest fashion events throughout the Middle East. Some of these events have spread to non–Middle Eastern countries. In December 2018, Seattle Muslim women hosted the first Modest Fashion Night in that city.

Face-covering is a controversial practice in many Western countries. Clothing that covers the entire body, head, and face is called a niqab or burka (or burqa). These are not fashion items but rather articles of purely religious clothing. Burkas would not be seen at modest fashion events and aren't featured by Islamic designers. In the larger Islamic world, the hijab is increasingly becoming a fashion statement and is incorporated with fashion. Zahra Lari is a figure skater from the United Arab Emirates (UAE) who began performing in international competitions wearing fashionable modest skating costumes that incorporate a head- and chest-covering hijab. Nike designed athletic wear for Muslim female athletes with its Pro Hijab project in 2017.

Ibtihaj Muhammad, a Muslim–American Olympic athlete, competed in the women's individual sabre wearing a hijab. She was later made the face of Nike's ad for their Pro Hijab project.

Who Is Halima Aden?

Halima Aden is the first Islamic supermodel to wear a hijab while modeling. Halima is Somali American and was born in a refugee camp in Kenya, moving to the United States when she was six. In 2016 she competed successfully in the Miss Minnesota beauty contest, wearing a hijab throughout the entire contest. She models for IMG.

TURKISH FASHION HISTORY

Istanbul is one of the world's great cities, considered a crossroads between East and West. It is still the largest city in Turkey. Along with other Turkish cities, it is a major producer of textiles for the home and clothing. Turkey has been a cross-roads for international trade in textiles since the days of the Ottoman Empire. At its height in the sixteenth century, under Sultan Suleiman the Magnificent, the Turkish Ottoman Empire ruled large portions of North Africa and the Middle East. Suleiman

A trader and a buyer both wear caftans and turbans at a market.

Today, in Turkey, fashion is a blend of Western and Eastern influences with some flair from the old culture.

was called "the Magnificent" because of his lavish clothing, which the rest of his ruling court also wore.

Ottoman Turkish men wore caftans—long, flowing robes made of silk or velvet and often trimmed with fur. They wore trousers, usually loose-fitting and tied at the waist and ankles. Ottoman Turkish women influenced world fashion in later generations because they also wore trousers, along with outer and inner robes. The sultan kept a harem comprising beautiful women in his palace, the legendary Topkapi, including a woman whose beauty and style was renowned—Roxelana, or Hurrem Sultan, the consort of Suleiman the Magnificent. Hurrem Sultan was a slave who rose to be co-ruler of Turkey with Suleiman, and her sense of style and luxurious clothing paled in comparison to her political acumen.

Modern Turkish fashion includes more than the red tasseled fez hat or harem girl trousers and cropped, revealing vests. The founder of modern Turkey, Kemal Atatürk, ruled Turkey between 1923 and 1938. He modernized Turkish clothing for both men and women, in addition to many social and political reforms. Fashion Week in Istanbul began in 2013 and features many Turkish designers who combine Western and Eastern influences in their designs, just as the nation of Turkey has throughout its history.

ALIA KHAN: FOUNDER OF DUBAI'S ISLAMIC FASHION AND DESIGN COUNCIL

Alia Khan exemplifies the new Islamic fashion industry, which has been growing throughout the Middle East since 2000. She has been named one of the 50 most influential women in the Arab world by *Arabian Business Magazine* and Entrepreneur of the Year by *Gulf Business News*. She is the founder and chair of the Islamic Fashion and Design Council, which leads fashion and design innovation throughout the Islamic world.

Alia was raised in the United States and Canada but has lived in Dubai since 2005. While in the United States, she had an independent media and marketing company with large corporate clients. Her combined experience allowed her not only to produce her own fashion shows but also to organize the Islamic Fashion and Design Council. The council sponsors fashion shows, retail and wholesale buying events, and cultural events in Dubai, Turkey, Kuwait, and European capitals such as Milan and Barcelona.

Actress Phylicia Rashad wore a design by Alia Khan during New York Fashion Week's "Heart Truth" fashion show.

In addition to the linens that have been found in Egyptian tombs, dresses made of beads were also made for mummies to wear in the tomb—a sign of divine representation and linked to resurrection.

PETRIE MUSEUM TREASURES

The Petrie Museum at University College London hosts some of Egypt's—and the world's—rarest and most precious fashion treasures. The 5,000-year-old Tarkhan Dress has a completely modern look despite being thousands of years old. It features pleating at the bodice similar to blouses of today and fitted sleeves. Curators believe that the dress was likely a funeral dress, as they've discovered two other similar linen dresses that are about 4,500 years old at Deshasheh.

Although not as elaborately stitched as the Tarkhan Dress, the "newer" dresses are 55 inches (140 cm) long: too long to be worn even as maxi dresses. All of the dresses were likely made for funerals of young women. Another ancient find includes 3,000-year-old detachable sleeves, which could have been attached to a child's tunic in cold weather and detached for hot weather. Each item looks completely modern and different from the ceremonial Egyptian fashion we are familiar with from paintings in pharaohs' tombs.

BELLY DANCE DRESS

"Belly dance" is a Western term for traditional Middle Eastern dancing, which dates to the nineteenth century in Egypt. The earliest belly dancers were a group of women called *ghawazee* who danced in Cairo in the 1830s. Their moves resulted in a ban from the city. The ban was too late, however, and their style and costumes caught on. Good belly dance costumes are designed for the dancer and hand-crafted, although many mass-produced versions are sold around the world.

Turkish belly dance costumes are among the more revealing, including a bra, belt, and skirt. Egyptian belly dance costumes are less revealing and include a gown instead of just a bra and skirt, because Egypt prohibits bare midriffs. Turkish costumes often include fringe instead of solid fabric for skirts, while Egyptian costumes have smooth-fitting skirts of solid fabric. Egyptian costumes also often include a veil. Persian or Iranian belly dance costumes include full-length skirts, tunics and jackets, and close-fitting trousers.

A display of belly dance costumes worn by Turkish dancers.

ARAB FASHION WEEK

Arab Fashion Week takes place in Dubai twice a year, in May and November. The event is sponsored by the Arab Fashion Council, which is a not-for-profit organization that has pioneered collaboration with international fashion in the Arab world. The Fashion Week

Designer Fatema Fardan walks out to applause as her fashion show ends during Dubai's Arab Fashion Week.

focuses on ready couture, a concept original to Arab Fashion Week. Ready couture is a form of ready-to-wear that can be customized to buyers and their taste and needs, entering a place in the fashion market between haute couture and individually made clothing and ready-to-wear mass-produced clothing in standard sizes. Ready couture may also be called demi-couture. Fashions on the runway at Arab Fashion Week can end up in ready couture boutiques of the designers that are featured.

Eli Tahari walks the runway with Christie Brinkley as she sports one of his famous pantsuits.

IRANIAN-ISRAELI DESIGNER ELIE TAHARI

Elie Tahari is an Iranian-Israeli designer who has established one of the most successful women's and men's ready-to-wear and accessory companies in the world. Tahari was born in Jerusalem in 1952 and emigrated to New York in 1971. He started as an electrician in New York's garment district but quickly gained notice as a talented designer. He is generally credited with marketing and popularizing the tube top, which enabled him to open his first store on Madison Avenue in 1974. Tahari also founded the mid-priced ready-to-wear design line Theory with Andrew Rosen. His clothes are tailored, elegant, and timeless. They have appeared in many television shows and films, including the sleek pantsuits and long coat worn by Gillian Anderson as FBI agent Scully in *The X-Files*.

CLOTHES FROM TUTANKHAMUN'S TOMB

The Tomb of Tutankhamun.

Clothing fragments from the Egyptian pharaoh Tutankhamun were found in his tomb in 1922 but were neglected for more than 70 years. In the 1990s, Dr. Gillian Vogelsang-Eastwood took on the project of studying and recreating 36 of the hundreds of articles of clothing found in Tutankhamun's tomb. The clothing ranged from striped tunics that the pharaoh probably wore on an ordinary day to a stunning gold-sequined tunic that he likely wore for ceremonial purposes. A leopard-skin robe and faux-leopard-skin shawl show that animal skins and imitations were common in Tut's time, just as they are today. The threads used for Tutankhamun's clothing were so fine that they could not be duplicated today, and modern substitutes had to be used instead for the recreations.

CONTEMPORARY UAE DESIGNERS

The Fashion Avenue atrium in the Dubai Mall attracts luxury-brand shoppers from throughout the Middle East.

The United Arab Emirates, in addition to Dubai, is a fashion center for the Middle East. The UAE is a good place for designers because of its access to trade, regional manufacturing, and textile centers. Known for her beanies, California-born Safiya Abdallah is now a Dubai-based designer whose clothing has been worn by Gwen Stefani. Abdallah is also a designer for Lohan by Lindsay Lohan. Twisted Roots is the brand of UAE-based Latifa Al Gurg, who has Emirati and Danish roots. Al Gurg's styles combine European and Emirati influences and emphasize quality fabric and fit. Marwa Sayed is an Egyptian designer who now showcases her work in the UAE. Sayed's ready-to-wear brand is Three Fifty Nine, which is stocked in the Emirates, Kuwait, Lebanon, and online.

CHAPTER 6 NORTH AMERICA

North America encompasses Mexico, the United States, and Canada and has a clothing history that dates back more than 10,000 years. New York City has rivaled Paris as the world's fashion capital since the early twentieth century, and the Canadian cities of Montreal and Vancouver are also world fashion centers.

NATIVE AMERICAN CLOTHING

The oldest surviving footwear in the world comes from Fort Rock Cave in Oregon, dating back between 9,300 and 10,500 years. Fort Rock sandals are made from sagebrush bark and are intricately woven to provide strength and durability. Like many other objects of clothing made by Native Americans, the sandals make maximum use of natural resources. Native Americans used plant fibers and cotton to weave cloth for blankets and clothing. They used natural dyes from plants and animal sources, including red cochineal, a dye made from tiny insects.

More than almost any other people around the world, Native Americans historically used animal skins for clothing, including bison and deer. Women were primarily responsible for tanning animal hides for clothing. Tanning makes the hides long-lasting and supple. Deerskin was often tanned with a solution made from the deer's brain, which contains lecithin, a compound that aids in tanning.

After animal hides were scraped or soaked in water, they were hung out to dry.

Native American woman I-ah-to-tonah of the Nez Perce tribe in 1909.

Before any tanning could take place, all the flesh has to be removed, as well as hair. The hides were the scraped or soaked in water to remove any remaining unwanted bristles and hair.

In warmer climates, Native American men often wore only breechcloths, a simple fabric covering for both front and rear tucked into a leather belt. Women usually wore skirts and leggings. Women in some tribes, including the Apache and Cherokee, wore deerskin dresses. Movies and books made the fully feathered Lakota, Crow, and Cree feathered war bonnet into the most famous Native American men's head-wear, but the feathered headdress wasn't the most common head covering for most Native Americans. Instead, this was the roach, a stiff porcupine strip worn in the middle of the head. The roach is the inspiration for the "Mohawk" hairstyle.

Contemporary Halloween costumes that interpret Native American clothing styles for the holiday are not only unrealistic and inaccurate, they are disrespect-ful to indigenous peoples.

THE GREAT AMERICAN BLUE JEAN

The earliest dyed fibers are 5,000-year-old pieces of indigo cotton found in Peru. The natural blue dye is the secret to the faded magic of blue jeans. Blue jeans are an American original, and anyone who owns a pair of Levi's jeans can read part of this history on the label: The jeans were patented by Levi Strauss and Jacob Davis in 1873.

The blue denim used for Levi's jeans originally came from Genoa, Italy, which inspired the name "jeans." Denim was a coarse, sturdy cotton fabric used by sailors in the Genoese navy because it could be worn in wet or dry weather. Women also wore dresses made from the material. Seventeenth-century paintings by "The Master of the Blue Jeans" show Genoese men, women, and children wearing faded jackets, skirts, and other clothing made from blue denim.

Levi's blue jeans displays are a staple in North American stores.

Calvin Klein continues to be one of the top brands for "designer jeans." In recent years, celebrities like the Kardashian-Jenner family have been the faces of Calvin Klein ads across the nation.

Levi's jeans were originally made for miners in California's gold country, along with cowboys, who were everywhere in the West. Rivets reinforced the original blue jeans at key stress points. Five-pocket button-fly Levi's 501 jeans remain a classic. Jeans were work- or farmwear for the next 80 years, until film legend James Dean wore jeans, a red windbreaker, and white T-shirt in *Rebel without a Cause*. Throughout the 1950s and 1960s, jeans were official youthwear. The styles worn by the actors in *Grease* were real-life fashion in American high schools.

By the 1970s, "designer jeans" became popular with men and women, starting with Calvin Klein's ads featuring Brooke Shields wearing nothing but boots and "Calvins." While Levi's remains one of the world's top-selling brands, nearly every American and world designer also offers jeans in various styles, including straight-leg, skinny, flared, or relaxed.

AMERICA LED WORLD FASHION IN THE 1920S

Fashion trends in the United States tended to follow European styles up until the 1920s, a decade when many things changed. Known as the Jazz Age or the Roaring Twenties, America suddenly became a world leader in music, film, and fashion. The Hollywood film industry led in many types of movies, and people were looking to revitalize their lives after the four years of World War I (1914–1918), in which millions of lives were lost.

American fashion for young women in the 1920s looked fresh, new, simple, and fun. It also gave women freedom from the restrictive, elaborate, and formal clothing of prior generations. Hemlines were shortened from the prim ankle or floor length of previous fashion—in some cases, to scandalously short lengths. Today's club dress has its ancestor in the silk sheath of the "flapper" from the 1920s. Instead of corsets lined with whalebone creating an artificial waist and uplifted bustline, the dresses of flappers were easy to wear and emphasized comfort and movement.

Although Parisian designers like Coco Chanel introduced elements of the flapper style, international fashion was now driven by Hollywood films. Early film stars

In the 1920s, hemlines in women's fashion were significantly shorter than they were in the decades before.

Bathing suits reached new heights in the 1920s, too. Pictured here, a beach official measures the hemline and the amount of thigh exposed by a young women's suit.

like Gloria Swanson, Mary Pickford, and Marion Davies showcased sleek new dress styles. Even Mary Pickford's girlish, wholesome image included simple short dresses with square necklines. The main style icon of the 1920s was the "It Girl," Clara Bow, whose cupid-shaped mouth, short hair, and petite figure made her the perfect flapper for the new age.

Along with the short, beaded, and fringed flapper dress, young women wore high heels routinely for the first time during the Jazz Age. Combined with short hair and an acceptance of trousers for women for casual or athletic wear (and the ability to vote), the women of the 1920s were among the first "liberated" women in history.

Katharine Hepburn, Trailblazer

Hollywood glamor was at its height in the 1930s with satin-gown-wearing platinum blonde Jean Harlow and classic beauty Greta Garbo. In contrast, Katharine Hepburn wore wool trousers, low heels, and tailored suits. Her sense of personal style fueled a film and fashion partnership with the legendary Hollywood designer Edith Head.

DUPONT SYNTHETIC FABRICS CHANGE CLOTHING FOREVER

The United States is the birthplace of synthetic fibers. A brilliant organic chemist named Wallace Carothers invented nylon, the first synthetic fiber, while working for the DuPont chemical company in the 1930s. Tragically, Carothers did not live to see the many uses for the material he created; he suffered from depression and committed suicide in 1937. Nylon is a plastic polymer that can be formed into thread, bristles, and many other materials. It is used in countless fabrics today, but when it was put on the market in 1940, it was in the form of nylon stockings. Few people wear stockings today, but before nylon became available, all stockings were silk, and thus too costly for the average woman in America or around the world.

DuPont shifted nylon production from stockings to war materials in 1941 because of World War II. That same year, British chemists produced the first examples of polyester fiber, but DuPont chemists in the United States refined the process and produced massive amounts of polyester fiber. Spandex was invented at a DuPont lab in 1958, serving as the basis for the majority of athletic and casual clothes sold worldwide today.

Spandex has come a long way since the DuPont lab. Today, spandex is used by many fashion and athletic clothing companies for sportswear. Yogis will often wear spandex as it does not restrict their flexibility.

THE COUNTERCULTURE FASHION OF THE 1960S

If the 1920s Jazz Age and flapper era shocked older generations, they certainly weren't ready for the fashion revolution of the 1960s. This was the first generation where streetwear influenced haute couture, rather than the other way around. From miniskirts made of repurposed blue jeans to fringed vests and bell-bottoms, 1960s youth culture led a world fashion revolution.

The hippies of this era weren't just influenced by psychedelic music and experimenting with psychedelic drugs. They were also interested in alternative lifestyles and cultures. Tie-dyed clothing, an ancient tradition in Indonesia and Africa, came to the United States in the form of brightly colored T-shirts and thousands of permanently stained bathtubs. Hippie jewelry included peace signs, love beads, chain belts, and shell necklaces. Both men and women wore bell-bottom jeans, and hairstyles that broke from the norm emerged. African Americans grew their hair and wore it naturally in Afro styles, while countless young men let their hair grow and wore it loose or in a ponytail.

The hippies of the 1960s often wore repurposed blue jeans, fringed vests, and bell-bottoms. Much of this fashion was seen at the 1969 Woodstock music festival.

MONTREAL, A FASHION CAPITAL

Montreal was named the most elegant city in Canada in 2017 by the global fashion retailer Zalando. Montreal's Fashion & Design Festival, held each year in August, is the largest outdoor fashion festival in the world, attended by over half a million people. The city is home to some of Canada's best fashion designers, including Denis Gagnon, noted for his experimental designs and materials. Other Montreal-based brands include the outerwear brand Mackage and menswear standout Philippe Dubuc.

The total sales of the fashion industry in Quebec were more than $8 billion in 2018, and the industry employed more than 82,000 people. Montreal is the third largest clothing manufacturing city in North America, after New York and Los Angeles. More than 1,800 businesses operate in the fashion sector throughout the province, the majority in Montreal.

A lingerie fashion show at Montreal's Fashion & Design Festival.

EDITH HEAD: HOLLYWOOD'S MOST AWARDED DESIGNER

Instantly recognized by fashion insiders for her round-rimmed glasses and severe black bangs, Edith Head is the most awarded Hollywood costume designer in history. Completely self-taught, Head began designing at Paramount with no experience. She created some of the most iconic costumes for Hollywood's most beautiful leading ladies for six decades, from the 1920s to the 1980s.

Academically gifted, Head graduated with a master's degree in romance languages from Stanford University in 1920. One of her first well-known designs was Dorothy Lamour's sarong dress in the film *The Hurricane*. She designed the iconic chiffon skirts and ballet tops worn by Grace Kelly in *Rear Window*, as well as Elizabeth Taylor's satin strapless gown in *A Place in the Sun*.

Edith Head's designs were featured on Grace Kelly in Alfred Hitchcock's Rear Window.

CALVIN KLEIN

Calvin Klein is the designer behind one of the world's largest fashion and lifestyle brand empires. Klein was born in New York City in 1942 and grew up in a Jewish family. His grandmother owned a tailoring shop, which contributed to his love for fashion. Klein's concept of using celebrities to market his clothing first achieved international fame with teen model Brooke Shields and her "Nothing Comes between Me and My Calvins" billboards and commercials in 1981. The most famous Calvin Klein underwear ads date from 2006, when soccer legend David Beckham showed off his physique in a pair of plain white Calvin Klein briefs.

Calvin Klein ads continue to be featured in large cities across the country.

RALPH LAUREN

Ralph Lauren was born to a Jewish family in the Bronx in New York City in 1939. He turned his preppy ethic and love of fashion into a lifestyle brand and fashion empire worth nearly $1 billion. Ralph always loved fashion and clothing, and as a young man in the 1960s he designed his own clothes because he couldn't find any that were elegant or tailored well enough in stores.

Clothing by Ralph Lauren can be found in major department stores across the country.

Initially, Lauren sold ties through the NYC clothiers Beau Brummell—appropriately named, as the designer was a twentieth-century "dandy," much like the store's namesake. Lauren sold $500,000 worth of ties during the initial season, and he soon added suits and shirts. The next year Ralph Lauren Polo launched, including the famous Polo logo. After more than 50 years, his lifestyle brands include Polo Ralph Lauren, Ralph Lauren, Chaps, and Denim & Supply Ralph Lauren.

New York Fashion Week brings the best fashion, and fashion lovers, to the city.

NEW YORK FASHION WEEK

Like other world fashion weeks, New York Fashion Week (NYFW) is a twice-annual week-long seasonal event that draws together professionals in the industry to promote fashion innovation. The event is one of four major fashion weeks around the world: the others occur in Milan, Paris, and London. New York Fashion Week has its roots in World War II. In 1943, event founder Eleanor Lambert, a publicity director for the New York Dress Institute, organized the week to promote U.S. fashion designers. By the 1990s, several fashion events throughout the city were consolidated into a single event. Formerly held in Bryant Park, NYFW has been held in different venues around NYC since 2009.

CHAPTER 7 OCEANIA

Oceania includes Australia and New Zealand, Papua New Guinea, Indonesia and the Philippines, Micronesia, and Polynesia, including the South Pacific islands and Hawaii. It encompasses some of the world's oldest cultures in Australia and Papua New Guinea, and the newest in Polynesia, which began to be settled around 800 BCE.

THE AUSTRALIAN FASHION INDUSTRY

Aboriginal Australians wore cloaks made from animal skins—reports that they wore no clothing are untrue. Cloaks for men and women were sewn from kangaroo, wallaby, and possum skin. They were pinned around the shoulders and waist and decorated by etching designs into the hide. Australia's fashion industry is now worth 28.5 billion Australian dollars annually, and it employs more than 37,000 people.

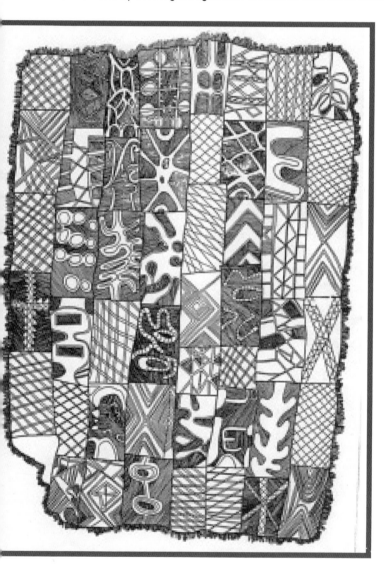

As a colony of Great Britain, Australia followed European fashion for more than two centuries after the First Fleet landed in 1788. Melbourne became Australia's fashion and retail capital in the twentieth century, with department stores like Georges on Collins providing stylish ready-to-wear clothes for Australian women. Melbourne also had several fashion boutiques, including La Petite, specializing in Paris-inspired fashions that included

Possum-skin cloaks, like this one, are on display in Museum Victoria's collection.

Australia's fashion and clothing has been influenced by the nation's seafaring and surfing heritage.

some Australian flair. A 1959 blue silk evening dress designed by Pat Rogers features a beaded bodice and a dyed ostrich feather skirt that echoed the emu cloaks of aboriginal Australians.

Australian fashion has always been inspired by Pacific Rim cultures and native designs, as shown by a 1935 dressing gown created by Annie Ellis Australia. The gown and other precious artifacts of Australia's fashion and clothing history are preserved at the National Gallery of Victoria in Melbourne. Australia's outback is reflected in the iconic silhouette of the bush-riding duster coat. The nation's seafaring and surfing heritage can be seen in its influential position in surf fashion and culture. The two largest Australian fashion and clothing companies are surf apparel and lifestyle brands Billabong and Rip Curl. Another well-known surf brand, Quiksilver/Roxy, was founded in Torquay, Australia, but is now headquartered in Southern California. Australian bathing suits for women are some of the best-selling and best-constructed in the world, thanks to Australia's extensive surf culture and world-renowned beaches, and led by the Seafolly and Zimmermann brands.

MAORI CLOTHING, JEWELRY, AND TATTOOS

The Maori are Polynesian people who arrived in New Zealand in the thirteenth century. About 730,000 Maori live in New Zealand. Traditional Maori culture is being revitalized, including the Maori language, jewelry, some forms of dress, and tattoos. Like other Polynesian peoples, the Maori made traditional clothing from plant fibers, animal skins (including seal and dog), and bird feathers. Traditional Maori menswear is among the most varied and intricate of Polynesian clothing. Capes and cloaks of different sizes and shapes range from rain capes to full-length ceremonial cloaks, indicating a man's status and role in society. The Maori also used many different local plant fibers and vines to create their clothing, particularly flax and cabbage trees. Cabbage trees are a palm-like tree that grows throughout New Zealand.

The traditions of Maori culture have been revitalized with its people using its language, jewelry, some forms of dress, and tattoos.

Maori body and facial tattoos are not merely decorative; they have personal, family, and tribal meaning. Ta Moko tattoos are facial tattoos that traditionally indicate heritage and ancestry. Kirituhi tattoos are body tattoos that have much more varied meanings. Tattooing, especially face tattoos, are not just meaningful to individuals because they represent their ancestral heritage—getting tattooed represents a rite of passage for both Maori men and women. The intricate designs include symbols that represent aspects of Maori life, as well as symbols unique to families. Traditional Maori tattoos were not done with needles. They were made using shark teeth or sharpened bones or stones.

Maori jewelry is made from natural stone, bone, shell, and shark, whale, or animal teeth. Jewelry can be purely decorative, but most Maori jewelry is ornamental and symbolic. Some Maori jewelry depicts spiritual beliefs and legends. Other Polynesians refer to Maori as the "whale-tooth people" because they made so many different types of jewelry from whales, ranging from sperm whales to orcas (killer whales). Neck pendants made from jade, greenstone, or bone called *hei tiki* or *tiki* are highly treasured.

A Maori man with traditional facial tattoos and jewelry.

FRENCH POLYNESIAN CLOTHING AND JEWELRY

French Polynesia includes more than 110 islands scattered over more than 1,200 miles (2,000 km) in the South Pacific. The best-known island in French Polynesia is Tahiti, which also has the largest population in the region. French Polynesia is the only overseas autonomous country that is part of France, following French colonization in 1880. Polynesian people arrived in Tahiti and the other Society Islands between 300 and 800 CE. Tahiti is a world tourism destination, considered to be a dream vacation or honeymoon location by millions. In addition to the islands' natural beauty, the spirit of the Tahitian people is clear in their traditional clothing and fashion, as well as the island philosophy of *aita pea pea*, which means "not to worry."

Tahitians wove cloth from bark—called tapa cloth. Tapa cloth could be made from pounded

Men and women in Tahiti use tattoos to express their ancestry.

Tahitian leis and grass skirts are similar to those worn in Hawaii.

pandanus leaves, coconut fibers, or bark from breadfruit trees. This cloth is beautiful but stiff. The *pareu* is a single piece of fabric that can be tied around the waist, shoulder, or neck, similar to a sarong. Both men and women wear *pareus*. Tahitians also make decorative fabrics and quilts using reverse applique, a sophisticated technique that reveals underlying layers of fabric instead of applying pattern pieces onto a fabric base.

Like the Maori in New Zealand, Tahitians use tattoos to express their ancestry, personality, and social position. The word "tattoo" itself comes from the Tahitian word *tatou*. Tahiti is also home to exotic precious and semiprecious stones, including black pearls, which grow only in oysters from French Polynesia. The lei and grass skirt familiar from Hawaii are also worn in Tahiti, as well as the muumuu, a Polynesian adaptation of long dresses worn by colonial women. Life has a slower pace in Tahiti, one of the world's most gracious and beautiful places.

Paul Gauguin

French artist Paul Gauguin was a friend of Vincent Van Gogh who moved to Tahiti in 1891 and painted dozens of paintings of Polynesian culture, especially highlighting the beauty and sensuality of Tahitian women. Europeans were stunned by the vivid clothing colors and exotic beauty of Gauguin's models.

HAWAIIAN CLOTHING

Hawaii was settled as early as 400 BCE by people from the Marquesas Islands, which are located in western French Polynesia. Hawaiian culture evolved undisturbed by Westerners until Captain James Cook arrived in 1778. Hawaiian fashion was changed irrevocably by European contact, trade, and missionaries. Although there are many native Hawaiian types of clothing, jewelry, and fashion, nearly every article has some European influence.

The Hawaiian shirt dates from the 1930s, when workers on pineapple and coffee plantations started wearing bright-colored Palaka shirts. The muumuu dress, a loose-fitting comfortable dress, started out as a "Mother Hubbard" dress imposed by colonial missionaries on Hawaiian women to provide more modesty than their skirts and shawls. Among the most famous examples of native Hawaiian clothing are feathered cloaks made from the feathers of live birds who were caught and released. Making a single cloak can take many years.

Hawaiians participate in the annual Lei Day Celebration.

PAPUA NEW GUINEA

Papua New Guinea (PNG) is located in Melanesia and is the eastern half of the island of New Guinea, located off the northern coast of Australia. The nation has been independent of foreign control since 1975, and the history of its people dates back 45,000 years. Native Papua New Guineans are descended from people who originally migrated from Africa in one of the earliest human migrations. More than 850 languages are spoken in PNG, and hundreds of cultural groups and individual villages have their own styles of dress and traditions.

PNG is tropical, and residents usually wear minimal clothing including *lap-laps* and *meri* blouses. The *lap-lap* is a waist cloth that has front and back flaps that are tied around the waist, very similar to clothing worn by many people in the Amazon, which is thousands of miles away but with a similar climate. The *meri* blouse is PNG's version of the muumuu; missionaries introduced it to the island for the same reason as the muumuu: to encourage women to cover their bodies.

Native Papua New Guinea women dressed in traditional costumes with color on their faces, necklaces, and large skirts for a Hagen show.

THE FILIPINO BARONG TAGALOG

The Philippines are sometimes considered part of Asia and sometimes part of Oceania—the islands are south of Taiwan and north of Indonesia. With 300 years of Spanish colonization, much Filipino fashion and culture is Spanish-influenced. One clothing style that began in precolonial times is the *barong* Tagalog, or *barong*, the Filipino national shirt that is primarily worn by men but can also be worn by women.

Barong Tagalog shirts are long-sleeved and worn loose-fitting over trousers. The shirts evolved from native Filipino tunics called *kangas*. The *kanga* had no collar, while today's Barong Tagalog shirts have a collar and placket/partially buttoned front. The shirts are made from a variety of fabrics, including many that aren't typically associated with men's shirts, like organza and silk. Filipino piña fabric is a traditional textile handmade made from pineapple leaf fibers. Most *barong* are semitransparent and are worn over undershirts.

Filipinos often wear barong *Tagalog shirts*.

Graduates from UCLA wear floral leis.

THE LEI

The lei is a garland of flowers, leaves, shells, and other materials that is worn throughout Polynesia. Leis may be worn for personal enjoyment, beauty, or to signify a special event or social status. Maile leaves are not only beautiful, glossy green leaves—a maile lei signifies peace and harmony. Leis may be worn around the neck and can also be worn on hats or draped in the home. Floral leis are common at graduations from high school and college, not only in the Hawaiian Islands but also in the mainland United States, particularly in California. A lei is given to welcome people to Hawaii or to a home and may also be given upon departure in the spirit of *aloha*, which means both hello and farewell.

TAPA CLOTH

Tapa cloth was an important textile of Polynesia for much of its history. Primarily made from paper mulberry bark, tapa cloth was created by pounding stiff bark until it was soft, uniform, and could be dyed and printed with decorative designs. Different Polynesian islands used different materials for tapa cloth in addition to mulberry bark. Hawaiians made more than 60 kinds of tapa cloth, which they call *kapa*. Tapa cloth is lightweight and strong when dry, but it has some disadvantages. As a type of paper, it can tear and lose its strength in wet weather. Tapa crafts continue to be made today, but it is no longer used for clothing.

A wedding tapa cloth from Polynesia.

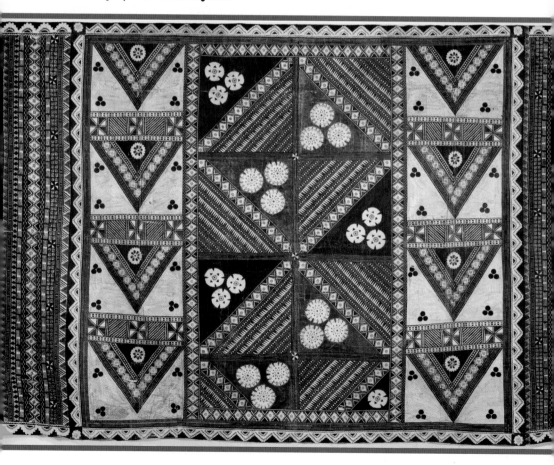

ARMOR MADE FROM COCONUT FIBER

Polynesians adapted the materials they found on the islands to meet their needs in many creative ways. The people of Kiribati, a group of islands in Micronesia, create coconut fiber armor—one of the most innovative uses of natural materials in the region. Kiribati islanders wove complete suits of armor, including body armor, back protection, a vest, sleeves, head covering, and leggings from fibers processed from coconut shells. The warriors who wore these elaborate costumes, which took hundreds of hours to make, carried clubs and tridents edged with shark teeth.

Warriors from Polynesia formed armor out of Kiribati coconut fiber.

BATIK FROM INDONESIA

Batik fabric from Indonesia inspired many similar techniques through the years, including Ankara cloth, which is popular throughout Africa. Batik is an ancient technique that is also used in Africa, but it is most associated with Java and other Indonesian islands. A wax-resist dyeing technique, Batik is made by applying melted wax to fabric in desired designs, then soaking the cloth in dye. All of the portions covered with wax will remain the same color they were before the wax was applied, whereas the dye colors the unwaxed portions. Complex designs and rich layers of colors can be built up through repeated applications of wax, dyeing, and wax removal.

A woman paints batik fabric by hand.

FURTHER READING & INTERNET RESOURCES

BOOKS

Croll, Jennifer, and Aneta Pacholska. *Bad Boys of Fashion: Style Rebels and Renegades through the Ages.* Toronto: Annick Press, 2019.

DK/Smithsonian. *Fashion: The Definitive History of Costume and Style.* London: DK Publishing, 2012.

LeLarge, Blandine. *Fashion Design Lookbook: More Than 50 Creative Tips and Techniques for the Fashion-Forward Artist.* Irvine, CA: Walter Foster, 2014.

McGraw, Sally. *Find Your Style: Boost Your Body Image through Fashion Confidence.* Minneapolis, MN: Twenty-First Century Books, 2017.

Rubin, Susan Goldman. *Coco Chanel: Pearls, Perfume, and the Little Black Dress.* New York: Abrams Books for Young Readers, 2018.

WEB SITES

https://afrolegends.com/. A multicategory blog about African heritage, including clothing, cultures, civilizations, music, and literature.

http://americanhistory.si.edu/collections/subjects/clothing-accessories. The Web site for the clothing collections of the National Museum of American History.

https://www.businessoffashion.com. Complete Web site covering the world fashion industry, from designers and manufacturers to courses in fashion history.

https://csdt.rpi.edu/culture/legacy/index.html. A multicultural Web site that provides math and design tools to create weaving patterns and projects, funded by the National Science Foundation.

https://fashionhistory.fitnyc.edu/. Comprehensive resource for fashion and design history from the Fashion Institute of Technology (FIT) in New York City.

http://www.historyofclothing.com/. A Web site with easy-to-understand articles about clothing, textiles, and clothing construction.

INDEX

adire fabric dye technique, 17
American fashion in 1920s, 74–75
ancient clothing, 14–15, 21–24, 26–27, 33–35, 46–47, 58–59, 70
animal fur and skins, 36, 47, 68, 70–71, 82, 84
Ankara fabric, 18, 93
Arab Fashion Week, 67
Argentina, 54
Australian fashion industry, 82–83

bark cloth, 10, 15, 86–87, 92
Barong Tagalog (Philippines), 90
batik (Indonesia), 28, 93
belly dance costumes, 66
Black Panther costumes, 12–13
blue jeans, 72–73
bowler hats (Bolivia), 53
Brummell, George "Beau," 43, 80
bustles and farthingales, 44

caftans (kaftans), 16, 63
Carter, Ruth E., 12–13
Central America, traditional, 46–47
Chanel, Coco, 39, 40, 43
China, ancient, 22–23
coconut fibers, 87, 93
colors, brilliant, 10–11, 18, 26–27, 35, 39
contemporary designers, 12–13, 19–20, 31, 55–56, 67, 68, 79–80
cosmetics (Ancient Egypt), 59
cotton, 26, 29, 47, 49
counterculture fashion, 77
Cuban fashion influence, 52, 55

de la Renta, Oscar, 45, 56
Dubai, 64, 67, 68
dyeing of fabrics, 17, 39, 72, 93

Egypt, Ancient, 58–59, 65, 68
Europe, medieval, 36–37

fashion weeks, 32, 63, 64, 67, 80
Folawiyo, Lisa, 19

Greeks and Romans, ancient, 34–35, 43

haute couture, 38, 67
Hawaii, 88, 92
Head, Edith, 79
Herrera, Carolina, 45, 55

Incas, ancient, 48, 49
India, 26–27, 29, 32
Islamic fashion, 60–61, 64
Italian fashion, 42

Japanese fashion, 24–25, 31
jewelry, 47, 48, 49, 77, 85, 87
Jones, Ikiré, 13, 20

kente cloth, 10–11
Khan, Alia, 64
Klein, Calvin, 73, 79
knits and knitting, 20, 35, 37
Korean hanboks, 30

Lakmé Fashion Week (India), 32
Lauren, Ralph, 80
leis, 87, 88, 91

Madiba shirts (South Africa), 19
Madras plaid (India), 32
Maori clothing and tattoos, 84–85
Mayans, ancient, 46–47
men's clothing, 11, 19, 20, 28, 43, 71, 84
Miele, Carlos, 56
Miyake, Issey, 31
Montreal and fashion, 78

Native Americans, 70–71
New York City and fashion, 69, 80
Ngxokolo, Laduma, 20

Pakistan, 26–27
pants (trousers), 21, 43, 63

Papua New Guinea, 89
Paris and fashion, 9, 38–39, 69
patterns, geometric, 11, 17, 18
Petrie Museum (University College London), 58, 65
politics and fashion, 50–51, 54
Polynesian peoples, 84–87, 91, 92, 93

ready couture, 67
ready-to-wear (prêt-à-porter), 41, 67
religion and clothing, 27, 30, 60–61

sarongs, 28
Savile Row (London), 44
silk, 22–23, 36–37
socks, 35, 37
South America, 48–51, 53–55, 56
status and wealth, 33, 36–37, 38, 42, 47, 49
synthetic fabrics, 76

Tahari, Elie, 67
tailoring, 44, 48
tapa cloth (Polynesia), 86–87, 92
Tarkhan Dress (Ancient Egypt), 58, 65
Tassili n'Ajjer rock art, 14–15
tattoos, 84–85, 87
Toledo, Isabel, 55
turbans, 26, 30
Turkish fashion history, 62–63
Tutankhamun's tomb, 68

United Arab Emirates, 68

warriors, female and male, 12, 43, 51, 93
women's clothing, 11, 19, 39–40, 43, 44, 53–55, 60–61, 71, 74–75
woven fabric, 10–11, 22, 32, 48, 58–59

youth fashion trends, 25, 31, 73, 77

AUTHOR'S BIOGRAPHY

Amy Sterling Casil has an MFA from Chapman University and a bachelor's degree in studio art and literature from Scripps College. She teaches at Saddleback College in Mission Viejo and Palomar College in San Marcos in Southern California and has published more than 26 books for school classrooms and libraries, as well as award-winning fiction.

CREDITS

COVER

(clockwise from top left) Bolivian Women in traditional dress, La Paz, Bolivia, Diego Grandi/Shutterstock; businessmen in traditional garb, Dubai, United Arab Emirates, oneinchpunch/Shutterstock; woman in Edwardian dress, London, England, KathySG/Shutterstock; Runway models during the Chanel Ready-to-Wear Autumn/Winter 2011/2012 show during Fashion Week, Paris, France, FashionStock.com/Shutterstock; blue jeans, Africa Studio/Shutterstock; kings wearing rich Kente cloth walking in state, Aburi, Ghana, Yaayi/Shutterstock

INTERIOR

1 Song Yang/Dreamstime; 2–3 Nitikorn Poonsiri/Shutterstock; 5 Dmitry Rukhlenko/Shutterstock; 9 Zvereva Yana/Shutterstock; 10 Yaayi/Shutterstock; 11 Yaayi/Shutterstock; 12 Faiz Zaki/Shutterstock; 13 Piu_Piu/Shutterstock; 14 Soukopka/Dreamstime; 15 Africanway/iStock; 16 Eric Valenne geostory/Shutterstock; 17 Olaniyan Olushola/Wikimedia Commons; 18 Alexander Sarlay/Wikimedia Commons; 19 (UP) Governor-Genneral of Australia/Wikimedia Commons; 19 (LO) Janet Mayer / Splash News/Newscom; 20 (UP) Dendenal/Shutterstock; 20 (LO) Stephanie Aaronson/Newscom; 21 AleshkaK/Shutterstock; 22 CRS Photo/Shutterstock; 23 Pablo Hidalgo/Dreamstime; 24 Studio Driehoek/Shutterstock; 25 SeanPavonePhoto/iStock; 26 Pavel Bulgakov/Shutterstock; 27 CherylRamalho/Shutterstock; 28 Keith Michael Taylor/Shutterstock; 29 Tottoto/Dreamstime; 30 (UP) zixia/Shutterstock; 30 (LO) Deman/Shutterstock; 31 (UP) Photographer253/Shutterstock; 31 (LO) FashionStock.com/Shutterstock; 32 (UP) Hindustan Times/Newscom; 32 (LO) Everett Collection/Shutterstock; 33 The tin man/Shutterstock; 34 Free Wind 2014/Shutterstock; 35 bparren/iStock; 36 Evdoha_spb/Shutterstock; 37 Tanja_G/iStock; 38 Haute Couture News/Wikimedia Commons; 39 Eric Koch / Anefo/Wikimedia Commons; 40 FashionStock.com/Shutterstock; 41 Siyapath/Shutterstock; 42 FashionStock.com/Shutterstock; 43 (UP) Robert Dighton/Wikimedia Commons; 43 (LO) Alfred T. Palmer/Wikimedia Commons; 44 (UP) Miiisha/Shutterstock; 44 (LO) Blueskynet/Shutterstock; 45 GeorgePeters/iStock; 46 Lena Wurm/Dreamstime; 47 Playa del Carmen/Shutterstock; 48 Cristina Stoian/Shutterstock; 49 duncan1890/iStock; 50 Wikimedia Commons; 51 Album / Prisma/Newscom; 52 The Visual Explorer/Shutterstock; 53 Vlad Karavaev/Shutterstock; 54 Everett Collection/Newscom; 55 (UP) Miro Vrlik Photography/Shutterstock; 55 (LO) lev radin/Shutterstock; 56 (UP) lev radin/Shutterstock; 56 (LO) Mariematata/Dreamstime; 57 Inna Makarova/Shutterstock; 58 Werner Forman Archive Heritage Images/Newscom; 59 Vladimir Wrangel/Shutterstock; 60 Sergei Bachlakov/Shutterstock; 61 Leonard Zhukovsky/Shutterstock; 62 Zniehf/Dreamstime; 63 Anna Krivitskaia/Dreamstime; 64 Slaven Vlasic/KRT/Newscom; 65 World History Archive/Newscom; 66 Nigel Hoy/Dreamstime; 67 (UP) Maksym Poriechkin/Shutterstock; 67 (LO) Ovidiu Hrubaru/Shutterstock; 68 (UP) Nick Brundle/Shutterstock; 68 (LO) Jborzicchi/Dreamstime; 69 Retro Clipart/Dreamstime; 70 BeeRu/Shutterstock; 71 Everett Historical/Shutterstock; 72 Silviya Arsova/Dreamstime; 73 TY Lim/Shutterstock; 74 Everett Historical/Shutterstock; 75 Everett Historical/Shutterstock; 76 Blulz60/Shutterstock; 77 Ric Manning/Wikimedia Commons; 78 Mario Beauregard/Dreamstime; 79 (UP) Dr. Macro, Paramount publicity photographer/Wikimedia Commons; 79 (LO) CatLane/iStock; 80 (UP) Sorbis/Shutterstock; 80 (LO) FashionStock.com/Shutterstock; 81 Retro Clipart/Dreamstime; 82 Lentisco, English Wikipedia/Wikimedia Commons; 83 Katerinasamsonova/Dreamstime; 84 Fotos593/Shutterstock; 85 Rafael Ben Ari/Dreamstime; 86 Stuart Perry/Shutterstock; 87 sarayuth3390/Shutterstock; 88 Yi-Chen Chiang/Shutterstock; 89 Michal Knitl/Dreamstime; 90 Artyooran/Shutterstock; 91 Joseph Sohm/Shutterstock; 92 Wayback Machine/Wikimedia Commons; 93 (UP) Ken Welsh/Newscom; 93 (LO) Adam Petritsis/Dreamstime